AFTER ALL

AFTER ALL

by

CLARENCE DAY

New York & London

ALFRED · A · KNOPF

1936

TO MY WIFE

Dearest, I am getting seedy,
Fat and fussy, kind of greedy.
If your love is on the wane
I can't reasonably complain.
Yet, since legally you're mine,
Try to be my Valentine.

Year by year, to my delight,
You have broiled my chop at night,
Made the toast, and filled my cup.
Oh my darling, keep it up.
Warm my slippers ere we dine.
Damn it, be my Valentine.

With acknowledgments to the Editors of the *New Yorker,* the *Metropolitan Magazine, Harper's Magazine, Harper's Weekly,* the *New Republic,* the *New York American,* and the *Saturday Review of Literature.*

NOTE

This is just what happened, except that I have left out about his swearing because he hated revision. I also left out how he swore at me when I balked at listening to the essays over and over again until one day he burst out, "Don't you suppose I hate it too? Don't leave me so God-damned lonely with it." Then we both settled down to work, feeling much better.

Clarence commenced to revise *The Crow's Nest* early last fall. Some of the essays he discarded; others he pruned carefully to get rid of the personal animosities, over-weighted sarcasm, and long-winded philosophizing. Most of all, however, he wished to get rid of the creaking mechanics of humor, such as parentheses, semi-comic explanations, and jocular asides.

As he weeded out essays he no longer liked, and shortened or rewrote others, he added a quantity of new essays, verses, and drawings.

When he began to survey the material he realized that the book was different somehow—fuller, broader. He decided to change the title. Even while he was sick he was trying to think of a new one. He said it was the first thing he would do when he got well.

"It's hard, though," he said, "to find a title, because, after all, it's just my way of looking at these problems and people."

KATHARINE B. DAY

July 1936

CONTENTS

Contents

Contents

AFTER ALL

FASHIONS IN LOVE

It's curious how fashions rule even love-making.

It seems natural enough that styles of clothing should change, and that old styles should look comic to us, but we are apt to think that this is due to the greed of dressmakers and tailors. Who is to blame for the astonishing changes that come in the ways we make love?

The fashion in vogue fifty years ago was for a man to approach a lady in a very delicate manner indeed, when he wished to embrace her. The next rule was that after approaching about half-way, he had to stop short. He had been trained to think that a woman was far too precious, too angelic, to touch. This must have made women feel nice and safe, but kind of desperate. When a girl had made the impression she wanted to upon the man of her choice, all he did was to moan in a resigned and musical manner and keep at a distance. That was why so many well-brought-up girls surrendered to a rake or a ruffian. They had learned that the principal aim of a high-minded man was not necessarily to win the beautiful creature he loved, but to sit in his room and have the right kind of gentlemanly sensations or vapors about her.

However, this was more true of the English than it was of the Scotch. The Scotch have never taken to all the English ideas of good form. They are hardy and valiant, they are romantic, but as a race they aren't fashionable. They admire handsome girls as much as anybody, and sing songs about their fine points, but even in the Victorian era they knew what they wanted. Fancies, no matter how delicate, weren't enough for them. They wanted the girl. If they couldn't have her, they yelled. Some of the most famous yells in literature have poured out of Scotland.

They didn't do a great deal of yelling, though. They were burly and cheerful. They never had such bad attacks of low spirits as men had in England. Usually a Scotsman got the girl, and then sang songs about how much she loved him.

One of the most famous English love lyrics is Lord Tennyson's thin little series of sighs, inserted as a song in his poem about "The Miller's Daughter." He says he wishes he were the girdle "about her dainty, dainty waist." If he were, he could hear her heart beat, he explains. It makes him quite excited to think of being able to hear a lady's heart beat, and apparently the only way he sees how to do it is to get himself turned into a girdle.

In the next stanza, however, he changes his mind. He gets thinking about "her balmy bosom" and wants to be a necklace instead. Then he could just rest there and "fall and rise" all day and have a fine time. This thought works him up into such a state that he becomes very daring indeed and says:

> "And I would lie so light, so light,
> I scarce should be unclasp'd at night."

The poem goes on for several stanzas, but the lyric part of it ends at that point, with this large bearded man presumably swooning away in bliss at the very idea of such ecstasy.

Then take Mr. Thackeray, for example. He can't very well wish he were a necklace, too, because Tennyson had that big idea first, but he's got to get on a lady's bosom some way or other. So he goes off by himself and decides that what he wants to be is a violet. That's even better than wanting to be a necklace; it shows that he's more ethereal. Necklaces last a long time, so of course a greedy old man like Lord Tennyson would choose to be something like that, but Mr. Thackeray has sweeter and purer feelings. He delicately avoids

night thoughts, too. He tells his girl that all he
wants of her, and the only kind of love-life he
asks, is

> "An hour to rest on that sweet breast,
> And then, contented, die."

If a modern young man were obsessed with the
noble ambition of being a violet, the family would
take him to a psychiatrist. Yet that was once the
right way to woo a lady, and it may come back into
fashion again, after the next war, perhaps. Some
gallant major-general will be found sitting on a
bench at the Battery, forlornly wishing that he
could be changed into his girl's coral lipstick.

Women have said and done plenty of silly
things, and they are worse slaves to fashion than
men, but at least they haven't made as big fools of
themselves as men in their love poems.

HENS AND GRAMMARIANS

A bloodless but angry battle has been going on for the last hundred years between grammarians and setting hens. As the hens themselves are too busy to fight, they have not taken the trouble to meet

the grammarians and deal with them as they deserve, but their faithful friends and owners, the farmers, have fought the war for them.

The grammarians contend that there are no such things as setting hens. If any setting hen were to appear at a grammarian's door and try to hatch eggs in his apartment, he would turn her into a sitting hen instantly.

He would point out to her that "sit" and "set" are now two different words. Originally, they both were forms of "sittan," a verb meaning "squat," which the ancient Saxons used when they squatted down on their haunches around the fire at night. Sometimes before "sittan" down they would "settan" their clubs in the corners. According to the grammarians, the ancient Saxons were quite fussy about this, and they used "settan" only in connection with an act done to something, whereas "sittan" wasn't an act they did to anything—it was just an act that they did.

Reasoning on this basis, grammarians point out that a farmer may "set" a hen if he wants to, but he mustn't then say that she is "setting," because she isn't. She is merely "sitting." Farmers argue that the purpose of language is to convey clear and accurate meanings, and a hen that is hatching eggs is doing a lot more than sitting.

Grammarians retort, "Look at Congress. When Congress is in Washington trying to hatch out some new legislation, nobody says Congress is 'setting'—we all say it is 'sitting.'" The farmer obstinately replies that hens are different. They work harder than Congress.

Extremists among the farmers have got so rebellious that they hardly use "sit" at all. When one of them wants to have a talk with his friends, he tells them to "set down and rest." Grammarians say that it's vulgar of a farmer to "set," even on a settee. The farmer complains that grammarians don't call all setters vulgar—English setters and typesetters, for instance. Why be so strict with a farmer? Grammarians will let him set a good example, or a clock, or his traps; he can also set his hand to the plow. Can't he ever set down?

No wonder these two words make trouble. You can "set" someone on to fight for you, but you must "sit" on him to stop him. After you have set a person at ease, you might think he could set at ease. But he can't.

It's not only farmers. Tailors bother grammarians too. Tailors say a coat "sets" well. If they say that to a grammarian, it makes him feel bad— or badly. (Some say one, some the other.) He tells them it may possibly "sit" well on him, but a coat cannot "set." A tailor in Bergen County, New Jersey, got so discouraged about this last year that he went out of business and became a sailor and is now setting sails.

The rule is simple enough; it's never to use "set" except with an object, but unfortunately the rule isn't perfect. To the intense annoyance of grammarians, like other rules, it has to permit some exceptions. One of the largest of these is

But the sun's an exception —.

the sun. He rises grammatically enough in the morning, but he sets every night. When the grammarians surrendered on this point, which they did long ago, some of them lamely explained that their rule was all right; it still applied to everybody and everything "except heavenly bodies." Others got out of it by decreeing a special dispensation, which now appears in the dictionaries, permitting us all to use "set" when it means "sink below the horizon." Anything to avoid fighting the sun.

A few grammarians are nowadays beginning to be lenient with hens, but these soft-hearted persons are denounced by the staunch old stand-patters. In order to please the strict ones, hens apparently must either become heavenly bodies or else learn to sink below the horizon before they can be called setting hens.

THE THREE TIGERS

As to Tiger Number One, what he likes best is prowling and hunting. He snuffs at all the interesting and exciting smells there are on the breeze; that dark breeze that tells him the secrets the jungle has hid: every nerve in his body is alert, every hair in his whiskers; his eyes gleam; he's ready for anything. He and Life are at grips.

Number Two is a higher-browed tiger, in a nice cozy cave. He has spectacles; he sits in a rocking-chair reading a book. And the book describes all the exciting smells there are on the breeze, and tells him what happens in the jungle, where nerves are alert; where adventure, death, hunting and passion are found every night. He spends his life reading about them, in a nice cozy cave.

It's a curious practice. You'd think if he were interested in jungle life he'd go out and live it. There it is, waiting for him, and that's what he really is here for. But he makes a cave and shuts himself off from it—and then reads about it!

Once upon a time some victims of the book-habit got into heaven; and what do you think, they behaved there exactly as here. That was to be expected, however: habits get so ingrained. They never took the trouble to explore their new celestial surroundings; they sat in the harp store-room all eternity, and read about heaven.

They said they could really learn more about heaven, that way.

And in fact, so they could. They could get more information, and faster. But information's pretty thin stuff, unless mixed with experience.

But that's not the worst. It is Tiger Number Three who's the worst. He not only reads all the

Book-lovers in Heaven

time, but he wants what he reads sweetened up.
He objects to any sad or uncomfortable account of
outdoors; he says it's sad enough in his cave; he
wants something uplifting. So authors obediently
prepare uplifting accounts of the jungle, or they

try to make the jungle look pretty, or funny, or something; and Number Three reads every such tale with great satisfaction. And since he's indoors all the time and never sees the real jungle, he soon gets to think that these nice books he reads may be true; and if new books describe the jungle the way it is, he says they're unhealthy. "There are aspects of life in the jungle," he says, getting hot, "that no decent tiger should ever be aware of, or notice."

Tiger Number Two speaks with contempt of these feelings of Three's. Tigers should have more courage. They should bravely read about the real jungle.

The realist and the romantic tiger are agreed upon one point, however. They both look down on tigers that don't read but merely go out and live.

THE OWL AND THE
PUSSYCAT

He did take her out for a sail in the moonlight one evening. But that certainly was not equivalent to a proposal of marriage. It didn't even show that his intentions were what women call "serious." All he meant it to be was an outing, an interlude, a romantic excursion. He had other work to do, other ties; he was an Owl, a philosopher, and she was not the sort of person that any of his family had married. He never dreamed that she might expect him to sail on forever.

But that was just what the Cat did expect, or at least engineer. A philosopher's wisdom is always at the mercy of craft.

They had barely left shore, in the moonlight, in a beautiful boat, and the Owl, overcome by the *mise-en-scène,* had but started to sing, when she snatched at his very first words to settle things. The female is cool. No *mise-en-scène* floods her with ecstasy. The rhythmical ripple of wavelets, the long shining path magically spread by the moon on the breast of the waters—all these leave a female as calculating as an expert accountant. The moonlight and waves are merely part of her office equipment. They are where she does business.

The Owl had taken out his guitar—a light guitar, you remember. Not a serious settle-down-for-life guitar at all, just a casual one. He looked up at the stars, an emotional thrill stirred his blood, and like many a victim before him, he burst into song. With the innocent idealism of men, he was led in his blindness to attribute the witchery of the occasion to the lady alone. He would never have sung to her thus with a guitar in the daytime, yet he let himself think it was she who was stirring his blood: not the night and the magical waters, no, only the Cat.

If he had looked at the cold, eager eyes of her as she sat in the stern . . . but unfortunately his gaze was on the stars. Only his words were of her. He attached no great importance to his words; they were the unpremeditated sounds of the moment: they were not legal instruments surely, with a red seal affixed. "Oh, lovely Pussy," he sang—as Samson once among the Philistines—

> " 'O lovely Pussy,
> O Pussy, my love,
> What a beautiful Pussy you are.' "

That was as far as he got. What lyrics he might
have gone on to, had she given him time, the an-
thologists never will know, for she at once interrupted. The female is supposed to inspire lyrics,
when in fact she aborts them. Her oily, insinuating
tones cut across his first twitterings:

> "Pussy said to the Owl,
> 'You elegant fowl!
> How charmingly sweet you sing!
> Come, let us be married.' " . . .

Marriage! She springs the trap instantly. Who
was talking of marriage? All he had said was that
she was beautiful, like the waves or the moonlight.
One doesn't, and can't, marry everything in sight
that is beautiful—one merely sings about them and
plays the guitar, a light instrument. Imagine the
stupefaction of this philosopher on a holiday jaunt,
to find that she was proposing to him and accept-
ing him all in one breath!

His song stopped abruptly. He had suddenly
learned Lesson Number One in the Book of Experience. From that time on he said nothing more.
He was much too discouraged. But, like so many
others, he had learned his lesson a trifle too late.

"Too long we have tarried," she continued.
(They had only just started, but naturally she was
in a hurry to get the deal closed.) She looked at his

wide, startled eyes through her own narrow slits, like a serpent hypnotizing a horrified but paralyzed sparrow. Then she too had a feeling of fright. There was a hitch after all. "But what," she cried in her dismay, "shall we do for a ring?"

This was Lesson Number Two for the Owl. He considered it silently. A marriage isn't real to a

woman unless there's a ring. She wants some kind of ceremony too—i.e., plenty of witnesses. It is part of the technique of lashing her prisoner fast.

For over a year she was unable to make him buy a ring anywhere. There are few shops at sea. The Owl had begun to have his hopes, perhaps, as she sailed grimly on, but it is a waste of time for a man in his position to hope. With the unerring instinct of the psychic, the Cat steered their craft to the land where the Bong-tree grows—a region not noted for jewelry, and yet "there in a wood a Piggy-wig stood, with a ring at the end of his nose."

The Owl had brought along plenty of money, as a man always must, even if he is only starting out for a sail in the moonlight. But either it was all gone by this time, or the Cat was most economical. "Dear Pig," she said (it must have been she who said it, for the cajolery is feminine; no male would go up to a perfect stranger and call him "Dear Pig")—

> " 'Dear Pig, are you willing
> To sell for one shilling
> Your ring?' "

No one knows what the Pig was doing there. A refugee probably. He blinked worriedly, his mind on escape. He looked at his brother in trouble, the Owl, and promptly betrayed him. "I will," he said briefly, thanking his luck that it wasn't "I do." The Owl was thereupon hurried away, and was married next day, by the Turkey who lived on the Hill, who was the nearest thing to a clergyman that could be found, and what a good eye the Cat had! A turkey is even better than a clergyman. He is more like a bishop.

The Owl was glad to get it over with; the Cat was triumphant. They ate an indigestible wedding breakfast, as prescribed by tradition—"mince, and slices of quince," nothing could be more dyspeptic than that—and the Cat inaugurated the petty thrifts of married life right at the start by allowing only one spoon for the two of them. Or it may have been merely her unhygienic sentimentality. And then, each thinking his own weary thoughts, they went back to the shore, and danced with the abandon of lost souls.

So the curtain goes down on them.

THE WOMAN'S SIDE

In vain, alas, the endeavor.
In vain she's tried and tried.
Her lord and master never
Can see the woman's side.

EDIBLE WORKERS

The great age of invention was in prehistoric times, long ago. The era we live in is also an age of invention—our stupendous achievements have dwarfed all the past, in our eyes; but naturally the inventions of old were more basic than ours. The inventions of writing, and wheels; the invention of zero, of needles, and wheat, and of money were made by great men. And aside from these, there were some highly ingenious devices which were made in a field we are wholly neglecting today.

Consider, for instance, the man who invented the cow. It is hard for us even to imagine a home without milk; but once it was very much harder to imagine homes with it. In prehistoric times it would have been easier for a husband to bring his wife orchids, if she had desired such weeds, than a bottle of milk. There was plenty of milk in the world, yes, but what was it doing? It was galloping around in the forest, in hostile containers. No thief could rob one of these animals without getting hurt.

Then a genius was born: a genius who experimented with animals, as we do with chemicals. One winter—by accident probably—he got an idea: the astounding idea of having milk at his door every morning.

The job was a hard one. To begin with, which was the best animal? Cows were far from the obvious choice. In some parts of the world men had tried to use the golden-haired ground-sloth, a coarse monstrous creature which they kept in caves and milked when they could. If they had succeeded we should have had sloths today in our fields, and our countryside poems and paintings would have been queerly different.

> The curfew tolls the knell of parting day,
> The lowing sloths wind slowly o'er the lea.

But the sloth was no good. Sloths have bad skin diseases in summer, they are wheezy at night, and every now and then there is a mean, fishy taste to their milk. These objections alone did not matter much perhaps in those days; but there was another, more serious: the sloth is monogamous. Commercially speaking, monogamy ruins a farm. When people found that every cow-sloth had to have her own bull, which the owner must tame, feed, and shelter, the sloth herds were scrapped.

At last a queer breed was tried out that looked even less promising. These were rough, horned, fiery beasts, running wild on the plains; as unlike our cows, almost, as iron ore is unlike a steamship. Yet that prehistoric genius saw in them first-class raw material for household machines that would manufacture milk every day.

People called him utopian, probably. Most inventors are laughed at. How did this one get help enough to capture those wild cows of old? It wasn't like digging for metals, which at least remain stationary. This raw material had to be chased, caught, and dragged home alive. And after he had slowly bred out their excessive mobility and speeded up the flow of their output, there was still much to do, before he could safely install them in the average household. Many users disliked being kicked while extracting the milk, and others complained, though in vain, of being gored by those horns. But with all its imperfections and dangers, this invention succeeded. It was a practicable and serviceable device for the production of milk, and with very few modifications we are using it yet.

Another great thinker in the meantime invented the hen. Instead of the tiresome search for small eggs in birds' nests in the woods, this epicure provided mankind with large eggs in the home. From all the many timid varieties of birds on our planet, he selected an odd, strutting breed and went slowly to work. He patiently coaxed these surprised birds to abandon the forests, reduce their wing wastage, and learn to go into production.

In our own Western Hemisphere, men invented the llama and turkey. In Asia they invented the camel, as a freight car or van. And one of Henry Ford's predecessors, several thousand years back, invented cheap and swift transportation by taming the horse.

Contrast these inventions with ours. How hard on us ours seem. They have added perhaps even more than the old to our comforts but, strangely enough, they have added far more to our toil.

If one of those ancient inventors could revisit the world, he would of course be much amazed by the wonders we've wrought. But he would be still more amazed at how hard we now work.

"There was nothing like this in my time," he would tell us. "Why on earth do you do it?"

"Well, you see," we should have to explain, "our inventions demand it."

He would blink at us and shake his head and look very puzzled at this. Perhaps, after thinking awhile, he would say, "I don't see it. With all the animal kingdom before you, to train and develop, I don't understand why you use for these tasks only men.

"In our day I wonder if we were not more resourceful than you. If one of our inventions grew tyrannous we did something about it. I remember, for instance, we had a lot of trouble with sheep. They bred far more rapidly than the specifications had called for, and they got out of order too easily and needed far too much servicing. But we certainly did not allow ourselves to be enslaved by our sheep. We were too self-respecting for that. We invented the collie.

"Why is it you don't man your coal mines with an improved breed of bears? If you can train wild horses to give up their kicking and biting and running away and become instead obedient carriers, reliable and gentle, you ought to find it comparatively easy to train the bear to mine coal.

"You couldn't put him to work in a mine as he is, I admit. But look at him as raw material from which you could make miners. He has strength and intelligence and a manlike way of using his paws. You could breed for still better paw action. What more could you ask? You have here a far better start than the original cow.

"But the last thing you ever seem to think of is using the animals. When one of your explorers finds a new species, notice what happens. He brings back a specimen, merely to put in a zoo. Or he brings home the skin as a rug, or to mount in museums. That's his only idea of a use for his new raw material. It is as though you had done nothing whatever with metals except to hang iron ore on your walls, or display bits in cabinets, or have photographs taken of yourselves capturing a stray chunk of copper.

"There are three great fields for inventors to work in, three kinds of material: animal, vegetable, mineral. Why don't you invent some new animals? You have urgent need of the discoveries you could make in this field. But—in this—you are not only at a standstill: you scarcely wish to advance.

"As a man of that great far-off epoch, the spirit of which you've forgotten, I am simply aghast at the way you men work in your world. How is it that men so inventive and resourceful as you, the creators of so much magnificence, consent to such drudgery? Everywhere I look I see battalions and armies of toilers, and still other armies are actually begging for toil. When I used to think, many years back, of what the future would be, how utterly unlikely and hellish such a scene would have seemed!

"I am, of course, still more amazed by your acceptance of toil. The high make the low work, and the communists try to make everyone; but nobody —not even the communist—tries to abolish it.

"Your inventors do talk of abolishing it. But look at their method. They invent new machines that will automatically operate old ones—and then design these new machines to be operated by men. Why must they invent all machines with human attendants in view? Why not at least try to design them for animal handling? Or why not invent better animals, able to run your machines?

"Why, if you moderns had lived in the days when the wheel was discovered, you would not even have thought of using horses, to judge by the way you now act. I believe you would actually have drawn your wagons yourselves. Yes, and you'd have kept dragging them patiently for thousands of years, until steam at last brought some relief to your toilers in harness. We men of old, whom you patronize, had more ingenuity. We invented the horse before the cart, and several other beasts too —mules, donkeys, oxen, and so on. We made the wheeled cart a blessing to men; you'd have made it a curse.

"There are plenty of species which you could use on your machines. And once you had schooled them to perform the same acts every day, you would have little trouble in making them keep on for life. Habit would be as powerful with machine-tending weasels as men.

"Human beings themselves are wild animals when they are born—more helpless than other species, but by no means more tame. Don't you realize if you can tame boys you can tame almost anything?

"There is no need to fear that trained animals would not do their work. A world that has seen simians learn to work will see anything learn. If some planetary steward could have directed the affairs of the world he would have made toilers of creatures that like daily toil. The industrious beaver, the busy bee, the hard-working mole. He would never have planned to have the world's daily toil done by simians. Activity, yes; but not drudgery. It is against human nature. No wonder it depresses and deforms you and leads men to strike.

"Some day your descendants will marvel at your wastage of animals, leaving the woods full of husky beasts idling about, while you nearly killed yourselves toiling, and grumbled at fate."

Let us open our eyes to the capacities and uses of animals. For instance, consider for a moment the question of language. We should need to communicate freely with our animal workers, and give them complicated instructions and warnings. Of course. But there should not be any great difficulty about doing that.

We cannot communicate freely with animals now. But this is because our whole attitude is too set about it. We have only one idea in our heads: make them learn human speech. If they can't learn to speak it, let them learn to understand it, at least. For thousands of years there we've stuck. Yet the solution is simple.

Who are the greatest specialists in languages? We, not the animals. Why should the poor creatures learn ours, then? Why don't we learn theirs?

Consider the dog. He learns not only dog-talk but a great deal of human speech also, so far as understanding it goes. But how little his master learns of dog-talk—only a few simple sounds. Unless a dog acts it out for us, we can't understand him at all. Dogs have learned to understand men, but men can't understand dogs.

We are adepts at learning several tongues apiece, when we desire to. Some of them are difficult, too: Chinese, Russian, Sanskrit. Why should learning bird-talk or dog-talk be impossible for us?

It wouldn't seem impossible at all if we cared about doing it. Suppose the whole course of invention had been the other way round, and we had invented all sorts of animals but almost no machines, and then suppose someone had suggested that we invent the X-rays, dynamos with thousands of horse-power, and a way to talk across seas. *That* would have sounded impossible. And yet we have done it. How long are we to let ourselves think we can't converse with the animals?

It won't be enough to learn the different animal languages. We should invent better ones for them. Scientists should make a thorough study of the speech organs of animals—their labial possibilities and limitations, their vocal cords and their palates, and the way canine teeth limit the swing of their jaws, as ours used to. Chart the vowel sounds and clickings and sibilants of which they are capable. Learn how they habitually use them to express what they wish to, and gradually devise ways to teach them to learn many more.

When animal workers talk, will there not be a risk of rebellions? It would be possible to answer this by saying that we have those already. Revolutionary animals would be dangerous, but less so than men. It must be admitted, however, that this risk is a real one. It is highly improbable that the animals would revolt by themselves, at least not in any well-organized or victorious way; but it is only too probable, unfortunately, that they would have human leaders, and not merely rascals or outlaws but noble idealists. All the bloodiest uprisings would doubtless be incited by persons with tender, compassionate hearts and cantankerous heads.

But humanitarians ought to consider the trend: the more elaborately the whole earth is organized, the surer it seems that the animals have only two choices—extermination or work. There is going to be no room here for animals that won't play the game. Their one chance of being allowed to survive in the future depends on how useful they are willing and able to be.

Think of great future factories where interested wolverines work, their eyes shining with happy excitement as they gallop about, pulling levers. Every morning a flock of eager woodpeckers will be seen in the sky, with an aviator herding them up from Navesink to their carpenter-shop work in town. Ferryboats for the employees of New York manufacturing companies will steam over from Jersey, full of chattering squirrels to tend bobbins. And parents of children will summon a kangaroo nurse-girl, slip the babies into her pouch with a sandwich, and send them off for the day. They'd be out of the dusty town in two jumps, and away to some sunny hill, watching the elephants haying or gathering fruit. There might even be night-schools or discussion clubs for the highest-grade workers—the Federated Grizzlies of America or the Order of Railway Raccoons.

If tender-hearted lovers of animals are afraid of this plan, let them hide for a month or a week in the jungle today, and learn whether animals are

happy there, or anxious and wretched. They may
well return shocked at how little the beasts have
to lose.

Idleness is not a blessing for many wild animals.
One famous hunter says somewhere: "I have often
heard great tragic beasts that cried in the woods,
like a woman, filling me with feelings of wonder
and pity at night." No wonder they cry. They want
work. They're neurotic without it.

Machines are man's new toy. He is so fascinated
by them, at present, that he wants to run them
himself. And no wonder. To control our most
powerful dynamos would thrill Thor or Zeus. But
as men have busily swarmed into their new ma-
chine-shops and factories, they have forced some of
their number to drudge until they are almost sub-
human.

So far from combating this situation by drafting
the animals, men's tendency so far is all in the
other direction. They have faced but accepted
their plight, and they even plan to breed robots.
Their objection to drafting the animals is that it
wouldn't pay.

If our modern civilization, instead of falling,
rose to new heights, would it pay? Let us bear in
mind how the great advances occurred in the past.
The old recipe for a high civilization was to have

slaves. There was no dispute as to that being necessary. The only disputes were as to just who the slaves were to be. The rich wished to sit on the poor, and the proud on the vulgar. If the poor and the vulgar were too fierce to let the quality sit on them, then both sides invariably joined together and sat on some foreigners. The Normans went and sat upon the English: result, a high civilization. The Romans sat on everybody: another. When the Huns wouldn't let the Romans exploit them any more—the Dark Ages. When abolition was forced on the South, the Old South went to pot.

Even if on the dollar and cents basis it wouldn't pay to use animals, it might save us politically and socially from going downhill.

But purely as a matter of business, why shouldn't it pay? It didn't pay at first to milk cows, but it has become very profitable. There would seem to be no limit to the profit a machine age could gain by using on its lower levels a new type of labor, that not only wouldn't strike for more wages but would get none at all.

The more that one studies human nature, the plainer it seems that the one crying need of civilization is Edible Workers. It is only when toilers are edible that they never grow old. At present the employer has no great financial incentive to keep his men ruddy and plump, and in fresh, sunny workrooms. At present there is suffering when he suddenly discharges his men. How happy a good employer would be with appetizing young workers whom it really paid him well to keep healthy when business was good, and whom he could lay off when he liked without anyone's suffering. In fact, it would be the other way round—there would be public rejoicing, and the employer would become a benefactor when he laid off his labor, and when nice young edible workers were sold at a discount. The unemployment problems of today would be instantly solved. In hard times there would be no more bread lines, but feasting instead.

Consider the cannibal. He used to devour captured warriors instead of broiled chickens. But as he grew civilized he lived on his fellows no more; he cooked other creatures, which he learned in time to make more delicious. A similar step should be taken by some modern cannibals. Men do not eat men but they live on them, they live on their labor, they use them for purposes quite as fatal to their existence. Are there no other creatures that men can exploit thus instead?

If we handled things rightly, the animals ought not to suffer. Men are kinder to animals, on the whole, than they are to their fellows. They select them more wisely, they fit their work more to their shoulders. They do not mistakenly stimulate the beasts' discontent. Using men as machine-tenders, they now educate them too much and surround them with incitements to be something more than they let them. But when they use animals they keep every beast in its place—they do not encourage their sheep to yearn, but to grow wool.

APE INTO MAN

A scientist evolved a plan
To turn an ape into a man,
But by the time that he had done
The ape was nearly seventy-one.
So all attempts to educate
The weary beast were rather late.

The ape, however, didn't mind.
He didn't wish to be refined.

THE SEQUEL TO IBSEN'S
A DOLL'S HOUSE

If a prize were awarded to the greatest love story, there might be many candidates, but surely only one would seem pre-eminent to a competent jury. Most of the famous love stories are entirely too smoky, too turgid. Abélard and Héloïse, Paolo and Francesca, Tristan and Iseult—none have the clear note of beauty. No, the noblest and best of such tales was written by a Victorian, a troubadour disguised as a jester—the good Edward Lear.

The characters in his drama are, first, Handel Jones, Esquire, who is the head of a great English firm. Second, his wife, Lady Jingly Jones, who does not like her husband. Third, a small, lonely hermit, with the heart of a Romeo or Leander, whose musical and mysterious name is the Yonghy-Bonghy-Bò.

An uninspired writer would either begin with the woes of the Joneses, or else he would have the third person insinuate himself into their home and plant complications. But why describe the old familiar details of an unhappy marriage? As well describe the spots in each case of measles—they are always the same. And why dwell on the complications of a triangle? That is quite as banal to free spirits, in spite of the ever-fresh interest taken in them by prisoners.

Edward Lear, being a man of genius, omits the whole business. He begins by introducing us, not to the man and wife, but to the true hero, the Other Man. And where does he ingeniously place him? Why, far off in the wilds. We are made to feel at first as though he were utterly alone in the world. He sets him before us so simply that we are attracted at once:

> "On the Coast of Coromandel
>   Where the early pumpkins blow,
>   In the middle of the woods
>   Lived the Yonghy-Bonghy-Bò.
> Two old chairs, and half a candle—
> One old jug without a handle—
>   These were all his worldly goods:
>   In the middle of the woods,
>   These were all the worldly goods
>   Of the Yonghy-Bonghy-Bò."

We hardly need to know any more of his nature than that. Compared to him, Thoreau on his river was a collector of bric-à-brac. The Bò had even fewer requirements than a saint in the desert.

But unlike the usual recluse he had no hard austerity; he was not a misanthrope but a warm-hearted lover of life.

Hence there comes that great day—once to every man—when he finds the right woman; and never has that poignant moment been more sweetly sung:

> "Once, among the Bong-trees walking
> Where the early pumpkins blow,
> To a little heap of stones
> Came the Yonghy-Bonghy-Bò.
> There he heard a Lady talking
> To some milk-white Hens of Dorking—
> 'Tis the Lady Jingly Jones!
> On that little heap of stones
> Sits the Lady Jingly Jones!'
> Said the Yonghy-Bonghy-Bò."

He is so intensely moved that he immediately springs into action. When an instantaneous recognition of the right woman is vouchsafed to a man, the right thing to do is not to shilly-shally but to wed her at once. "Will you come and be my wife?" he begs:

> " 'I am tired of living singly—
> On this coast so wild and shingly.' "

He tells her in the first place how happy she would make him; and then, in the second, to reassure any womanly doubts of hers about what they can live on, he describes how plentiful the food is in Coromandel—at least the shrimps, prawns, and watercresses. In addition he offers her all his possessions. He holds nothing back:

> " 'You shall have my chairs and candle,
>   And my jug without a handle!' "

And for occupation she and he can gaze on the rolling deep, he suggests. "As the sea, my love is deep," he adds quietly, and awaits her reply.

She is entranced. Who would not be? She has already perceived that he is the ideal lover for whom all women long. But imagine her anguish. To marry this dear hermit is a happiness that she cannot have—she has forfeited the right to it by already having a husband.

> "Lady Jingly answered sadly,
>   And her tears began to flow—
>   'Your proposal comes too late,
>   Mr. Yonghy-Bonghy-Bò!
> I would be your wife most gladly'
>   (Here she twirled her fingers madly)
>   'But in England I've a mate!
>   Yes! you've asked me far too late,
>   For in England I've a mate,
>   Mr. Yonghy-Bonghy-Bò!' "

England seems a far-away place to the Bò, but

Lady Jingly is tied to it. She describes her incumbrance and how he is always sending Dorking hens to her. He must have been an affectionate man, for he delights to do this, it seems. She says if he sends her any more she will give the Bò three of them. A woman of finer sensibilities would hardly have made such an offer, but wives get callous in married life and don't realize that lovers are sensitive. Yet she means to be considerate of the Bò and his feelings—she will not let herself play with them. She sends him away. She wishes she didn't have to say it, she tells him, but

> " 'Will you please to go away?
> That is all I have to say,
> Mr. Yonghy-Bonghy-Bò.' "

He goes. It is over. His one crowded hour of love-life is dead. Down the slippery slopes of myrtle he flees to the bay, and there he finds "a large and lively Turtle" on which he departs.

> "Through the silent-roaring ocean
> Did the Turtle swiftly go;
> Holding fast upon his shell
> Rode the Yonghy-Bonghy-Bò.
> With a sad primæval motion
> Towards the sunset isles of Boshen
> Still the Turtle bore him well.
> Holding fast upon his shell,

The Sequel to Ibsen's A Doll's House

'Lady Jingly Jones, farewell!'
Sang the Yonghy-Bonghy-Bò."

There's our clear note of beauty. Lohengrin on his swan and the Bò on his turtle—those are the two finest lyrics.

When Ibsen wrote the *Doll's House* his fame spread round the world. But long before the *Doll's House* was written, Lear give us this sequel. Ibsen's play ended with Nora's going out of the door to achieve independence. Lear shows us what she did with it: nothing—except to wreck one more life. But the Bò had so manly a spirit his life hardly seems wrecked, as he sails away into the sunset, singing that longing farewell.

And then in the last scene of all, we are given a glimpse of the woman. As the Bò disappears on the horizon, Lear turns back our eyes, and shows us that small huddled figure alone on her stones, weeping into a jug without a handle, among the incurious hens.

THE RABBITS CONQUER
FEAR

After the rabbits learned English, one of them found a popular book, called *Inspirational Talks*. He told several others about it. They were deeply impressed. Soon the rabbits assembled by thousands, in Australia for instance, to listen to an evangelistic rabbit read from this stirring book.

"Fear is your Greatest Enemy," he began, on page one. The rabbit audience fell into utter silence when they heard that. It was true. This book, although written for men, evidently could also teach rabbits. They waited most anxiously to hear how they ought to fight fear.

"What is Fear?" the preacher read. "Only a sort of Ghost. It is Nothing. But it is no less terrible for all that. For think what it does!

"It is this Ghost that knocks the Cup of Success from your lips, just when you are about to drink. It is Fear that unstrings your nerves, and pours its Senile Impotence into your heart.

"You have one Big Battle in Life. It is to conquer Fear."

This was the end of Chapter One. The book was printed in such very large type and had so many capitals in it that its chapters were short.

A rabbit organist played a hymn. The rabbits all stood up and sang:

> To him whose inmost thoughts are bright
> There's no such word as fail,
> No cruel foe he dreads to fight,
> No height he cannot scale.

> Then free your heart and learn to bring
> Your courage into play.
> You can ordain yourself a King
> And win your war today.

The leading rabbit stepped forward again and began Chapter Two.

"How can we get rid of Fear? Let us take some plain simple measures of common sense. Let us use our Will Power and Brains to attack this Foe.

"Rule One: If you are afraid of anything, walk right up to it!"

The audience shivered. "Even to a dog?" a little rabbit whispered in awe.

The rabbit preacher stood as tall as he could stretch, and his round pink eyes glowed. "Yes!" he shouted.

"Even to a very large dog, sir?"

"Walk right up to it," the preacher repeated, "and your Terror will be Gone. You will Laugh!

"Nothing is so bad when you get to it. It is foolish to worry. 'I have seen a lot of troubles in my day,' said an old man, 'and most of them never happened.'

"Repeat the formula of Courage. Say 'I can.' Be self-sufficient.

"There is just one person who is going to make you or undo you, and that is—You."

"I thought it was dogs," said the small rabbit nervously. But everybody said, "Shhh!"

"If you Fear anything," the preacher continued, "examine it carefully. Analyze it."

The small rabbit looked puzzled.

"It is the Unknown, not the Known, that throws you into a panic. Hence, whatever you fear, sit down and master it in your mind. Drag the Dreaded Thing out into the Light.

"And the second great rule is simply: 'Think Cosmic Thoughts.' You were born for some purpose. You are needed in the universal scheme as much as the tree is needed, or the star."

"Even in Australia?" asked one old rabbit doubtfully, from among the great multitude.

"That's what this book says," the preacher replied. "And now I come to the last page of all.

Think right about the Universe, it says. The Universe is your Friend."

The organist played another hymn, and the rabbits dispersed. The small rabbit, who was very impressionable, hurried off down the road toward a kennel, saying boldly to himself, "Drag the Dreaded Thing out into the Light."

ELECTIONS BY JURY

The other day, in a page of editorials, I found two crying evils which the editor was holding up under our noses to look at. (To smell of them was more his idea. He said they smelled to heaven.) One evil was the apathy the public displays at elections. The other was the excessive interest this same public shows at a murder trial. The editor was angrily pointing out that this was deplorable, and that he and his newspapers, therefore, felt bound to deplore it. He went even farther and said something ought to be done right away. But the only suggestion he could think of was that the public should change.

If that can be managed, it will solve the whole problem, of course. But in case the editor doesn't find it practicable to change human nature it might be a good idea to change our arrangements instead. One simple solution would be not to decide murder trials by a jury but by popular vote. And not decide elections by popular vote but by a jury.

We won't read political speeches that run over

a paragraph, but we eagerly read pages and pages of murder-trial testimony. We argue about a murder even at breakfast. The first thing in the morning we are trying to figure out who is guilty. But who seeks the solution at breakfast of a political muddle? And a lot of people won't go to the polls merely to vote at elections, but they would ask nothing better than to have a say about a good murder.

"Voting heavy on the Hall-Mills murder case," the papers would say. "Early returns indicate that Senator Simpson is guilty by a majority of 31,000,-000." If there were a delay of twenty-four hours or so, while country districts were heard from, that would be all the better, because it would prolong the suspense and make the occasion more thrilling.

On the other hand consider the advantages of deciding an election by jury. The jury system is only a makeshift way of deciding a murder case, but as a method of settling elections it is simply ideal. Every year, instead of putting the whole country at the mercy of orators, a number of men would be chosen by lot to listen for all the electorate. These human sacrifices would be locked up in a lecture hall and kept there throughout the campaign, and every candidate would be given a key so that he could go in and make speeches to them. He wouldn't have to wear out his throat either, as he does now, making the same old speech over and over—unless he himself wished to. If he did, he would, of course, have that privilege, but as a compensation to the jury for their hardships they could be pensioned for life. Even with this expense added, a campaign would cost far less than now.

Each juryman would see every candidate as well as hear all his arguments. That would make the new custom more thorough. It would be democratic, yet dignified. And on Election Day, instead of thousands of polling places, voting machines, clerks, and watchers, and a long and elaborate count of the whole nation's ballots, the jury would merely retire for an hour or so and announce the result.

PASSIVE RESISTANCE

A monk, believing God had meant
All flowers to be innocent,
Became peculiarly obsessed
    By one, too fully blown,
Which looked a little like Mae West
    And which he longed to own . . .

Passive Resistance

But sins can always be evaded
　By those who know their snares.
He stood and watched it till it faded—
　And then resumed his prayers.

A MAN GETS UP IN THE MORNING

A man gets up in the morning and looks out at the weather, and dresses, and goes to his work, and says hello to his friends, and plays a little pool in the evening and gets into bed. But only a part of him has been active in doing all that. He has a something else in him—a wondering instinct—a "soul." Assuming he isn't religious, what does he do with *that* part of him?

He usually keeps that part of him asleep if he can. He doesn't like to let it wake up and look around at the world, because it asks awful questions—about death, or truth—and that makes him uncomfortable. He wants to be cheery and he hates to have his soul interfere. The soul is too serious and the best thing to do is to deaden it.

Humor is an opiate for the soul, says Francis Hackett. Laugh it off: that's one way of not facing a crisis. Sentimentality, too, drugs the soul; so does business. That's why humor and sentimentality and business are popular.

A Man Gets Up in the Morning

The Russians whom we meet in Dostoievsky and Tolstoy are different. Men of that kind are not business-like, and they're not sentimental, or humorous. They are spiritually naked by contrast. An odd, moody people. We look on, well wrapped-up, and wonder why they shiver at life.

"My first interest," a Karamazov explains, "is to know where I stand: I must look at the past, and the seas of space about me, and the intricate human drama on this little planet. Before I can attend to affairs, or be funny, or tender, I must know whether the world's any good. Life may all be a fraud."

The Englishman and the American answer that this is not practical. They don't believe in anyone's sitting down to stare at the Sphinx. "That won't get you anywhere," they tell him. "You must be up and doing. Find something that interests you, then do it, and—"

"Well, and what?" Karamazov inquires.

"Why—er—and you'll find out as much of the Riddle in that way as any."

"And how much is that?"

"Why, not so very damn much perhaps," we answer. "But at least you'll keep sane."

"Why keep sane?" says Karamazov. "If there is any point to so doing I should naturally wish to. But if one can't find a meaning to anything, what is the difference?"

The American and the Englishman purse their lips. This isn't healthy. They look at him anxiously and continue to recommend business.

TO PHOEBE

"It has recently been discovered that one of the satellites of Saturn, known as Phoebe, is revolving in a direction the exact contrary of that which all known astronomical laws would have led us to expect. English astronomers admit that this may necessitate a fundamental revision of the nebular hypothesis."—*Weekly paper.*

> Phoebe, Phoebe, whirling high
> In our neatly-plotted sky,
> Listen, Phoebe, to my lay:
> Won't you whirl the other way?
>
> All the other stars are good
> And revolve the way they should.
> You alone, of that bright throng,
> Will persist in going wrong.
>
> Never mind what God has said—
> We have made a Law instead.
> Have you never heard of this
> Neb-u-lar Hy-poth-e-sis?
>
> It prescribes, in terms exact,
> Just how every star should act.
> Tells each little satellite
> Where to go and whirl at night.

To Phoebe

Disobedience incurs
Anger of astronomers,
Who—you mustn't think it odd—
Are more finicky than God.

So, my dear, you'd better change.
Really, we can't rearrange
Every chart from Mars to Hebe
Just to fit a chit like Phoebe.

Where the doteril cries

STRUGGLES WITH POETRY

There's nothing so indigestible as poetry when a reader is not in the mood for it. And even when he is it isn't easy to find the right poems. I'm always barking my shins on some masterpiece that is wildish and weird:

> "Go now from the shore,
> Far ruined: the grey shingly floor

To thy crashing step answers, the doteril cries,
And on dipping wing flies:
'Tis their silence!"

That sort of thing doesn't do a person like me any good. I stumbled on it just now in Ward's *English Poets*. It's by an inmate named Dixon.

I went on to read about Browning's father being a banker. Poor old man, I felt sorry for him. Imagine the long years when he and his son faced each other, the old father telling himself hopefully, "Ah, well, he's a child, he'll get over these queer poetical ways,"—and then his *not* getting over them, but proposing to give his life to poetry! Make a career of it!

If there are any kind of men who want sons like themselves, it's our bankers: they have their banks to hand on, and they long to have nice banker babies. But it seems they are constantly begetting impossible infants. Cardinal Newman for instance: his bewildered father too was a banker. Fate takes a special pleasure in tripping these worthy men up.

Imagine Browning senior studying *Pippa Passes,* with his ledgers around him. What mental pictures of his son's heroine did the old gentleman form, as he followed her on her now famous walk through that disreputable neighborhood? And what did he think of that poem where the man says, while galloping fast down the road:

"I turned in my saddle and made the girths tight,
  Then shortened each stirrup, and set the pique right,
  Rebuckled the check-strap, chained slacker the bit—"

Putting Browning aside I next had a try at Matthew Arnold.

The Arnolds: a great family, afflicted with an unfortunate strain. Unusually good qualities,—but they felt conscientious about them.

If Matthew Arnold had only been born into some other family! If he had only been the son of C. S. Calverley or Charles II, for instance.

He had a fine mind, and he and it matured early. Both were Arnold characteristics. But so was his conscientiously setting himself to enrich

He made the girths tight

his fine mind "by the persistent study of 'the best that is known and thought in the world.'" This was deadening. Gentlemen who teach themselves just how and what to appreciate, take half the vitality out of their appreciation thereafter. They go out and collect all "the best" and bring it carefully home, and faithfully pour it down their throats—and get drunk on it? No! It loses its lift and intoxication, taken like that.

An aspiring concern with good art is supposed to be meritorious. People "ought" to go to museums and concerts, and they "ought" to read poetry. It is a mark of superiority to have a full supply of the most correct judgments.

This doctrine is supposed to be beyond discussion, Leo Stein says. "I do not think it is beyond discussion," he adds. "It is more nearly beneath it. . . . To teach or formally to encourage the appreciation of art does more harm than good. . . . It tries to make people see things that they do not feel. . . . People are stuffed with appreciation in our art galleries, instead of looking at pictures for the fun of it."

Those who take in art for the fun of it, and don't fake their sensations, acquire an appetite that it is a great treat to satisfy. And by and by, art becomes as necessary to them as breathing fresh air.

To the rest of us, art is only a luxury: a dessert, not a food.

Some poets have to struggle with a harsh world for leave to be poets, like unlucky peaches trying to ripen north of Latitude 50°. Coventry Patmore by contrast was bred in a hot-house. He was the son of a man named Peter G. Patmore, who, unlike most fathers, was willing to have a poet in the family. In fact he was eager. He was also, unfortunately, helpful, and did all he could to develop in his son "an ardor for poetry." But ardor is born, not cooked. A watched pot never boils. Nor did Patmore. He had many of the other good qualities that all poets need, but the quality Peter G. planned to develop in the boy never grew. Young Patmore studied the best Parnassian systems, he obeyed the best rules, he practiced the right spiritual calisthenics, took his dumb-bells out daily: but he merely proved that poetry is not the automatic result of going through even the properest motions correctly.

Still he kept on, year by year, and the results were impressive. Many respected them highly. Including their author.

He grew old in this remarkable harness. Perhaps he also grew tired. At any rate, at sixty-three he "solemnly recorded" the fact that he had finally finished "his task as a poet." He lived for about ten years more, but the remainder was silence. "He had been a practicing poet for forty-seven years," Edmund Gosse says, as though he were describing a dentist.

One of this worthy Mr. Patmore's most worthy ideas was that the actual writing of verse was but a part of his job. Not even professional poets, he felt, should make it their chief occupation. No; one ought to spend months, maybe years, meditating on everything, in order to supply one's soul with plenty of suitable thoughts—like a tailor im-

porting fine woolens to accumulate stock. And
even with the shelves full, one ought not to work
till just the right hour.

His theories called for a conscientious inspec-
tion of each inspiration. They also obliged this
good gentleman to exercise self-control. Many a
time when he wanted to work he held back. Although "the intention to write was never out of
his mind" (Mr. Gosse says), Mr. Patmore had "the
power of will to refuse himself the satisfaction of
writing, except on those rare occasions when he felt
capable of doing his best."

There once was a man I knew, who wooed his
fiancée on those terms. He used to sit thinking
away in his library, evenings, debating whether he
had better go see her, and whether he was at his
best. And after fiddling about in a worried way
between yes and no, he would sometimes go
around only to find that she would not see *him*.
I think that she loved the man, too, or was ready
to love him. "His honesty has a horrible fascina-
tion for me," I remember her saying, "but when
he has an impulse to kiss me—and I see him stop
—and look as though he were taking his temperature with a thermometer first, trying to see if his
blood is up—I want to hit him and scream!"

Mr. Patmore, however, was very firm about this
being necessary. He had many a severe inner

struggle because of his creed. He would repulse
the most enticing inspiration, if his thermometer
wasn't at just the right figure. Neither he nor his
inspirations were robust, but they were evenly
matched, and they must have wrestled obstinately
and often in the course of his life, and pushed each
other about and exchanged slaps and tense bloodless pinches. But whenever Mr. Patmore felt it his
duty to wrestle, he won.

He took his temperature first

Consequently, looking backward he felt able to say when he was old: "I have written little, but it is all my best; I have never spoken when I had nothing to say, nor spared time nor labor to make my words true. I have respected posterity, and should there be a posterity which cares for letters, I dare to hope that it will respect me."

That last phrase has a manly ring. Imagine him, alone late at night, trying to sum up his life, and placing before us what bits he had managed to do before dying. We may live through some evening of that sort ourselves, by and by. We may turn to look back at the new faces of the young men and women who will some day be inheriting our world as we go out its gate. Will they laugh at us and think us pompous, as some of us regard Mr. Patmore? He doesn't seem very hopeful, by the way, about our caring for letters, but he does seem to think, if we do, that we will not make fun of him.

I don't think he ought to mind that, though, if we are friendly about it. We certainly respect him compared with many men of his time—the shifty politicians, the vicious or weak leaders of thought, who went through life as softies, without rigid standards of conduct. He shines out by contrast, this incorruptible, solemn old Roman.

Only—he was so solemn! "From childhood to

the grave" he thought he had "a mission to perform," with his poems. And what was this mission that he was so determined to fill? "He believed himself to be called upon to celebrate Nuptial Love."

Again it is his solemnity one smiles at, but not his idea. Nuptial Love? Very good. The possibilities of episodic love have been hotly explored, its rights have been defended, its spiritual joys have been sung. But Nuptial Love, our queer breed of simians, inconstant at heart, believes to be a tame thing by contrast: nearly all anti-climax. There are delights at the beginning, and a gentle glow (perhaps) at the end: for the rest it is a long dusty journey of which the less said the better. Exceptional couples who do somewhat better than this, and not only get along without storms but live contentedly too, are apt to congratulate themselves and call their lives a success. Contentedly! Pah! Content with mere absence of friction! No conception, apparently, of the increasing delight two should find, who devote themselves deeply to each other for all of their lives. I don't say this often is possible: I think people try: but one or the other comes up against a hard place and stops. Only, sometimes it's not that which prevents going further; it's a waywardness that will not stick to any one mine to get gold. A man slips away and runs about, picking up stray outcroppings, but loses the rich veins of metal, far down in the earth.

Why is it that so few of us contentedly stick to one mate, and say to ourselves, "Here is my treasure; I will seek all in her."

But Nuptial Love is not my theme, it's my friend Mr. Patmore's, whose spirit has been standing indignantly by, as I wrote, as though it were ordering me away, with a No Trespassing look. I will therefore withdraw, merely adding that he himself didn't do any too well with it.

However, no poet can avoid an occasional slump. For all Mr. Patmore's efforts, he needs to be edited as much as the rest of them. Take this stanza, from his poetical flight entitled "Tamerton Church Tower":

> "I mounted, now, my patient nag,
>   And scaled the easy steep;
> And soon beheld the quiet flag
>   On Lansom's solemn Keep.
> But he was writing jokes for *Punch*;
>   So I, who knew him well,
> Deciding not to stay for lunch,
>   Returned to my hotel."

May I ask why such verses should be enshrined in a standard collection of poetry? The last four lines are good, they have a touch of humor or lightness, perhaps; but what can be said for the first four? And they, only, are Patmore's. The last four I added myself, in an effort to help.

Some readers take to poetry as to music, because it enraptures the ear. Others of us feel a need for its wisdom and insight—and wings. It deepens our everyday moods. It reminds us of Wonder. Here we are, with our great hearts and brains, descended from blind bits of slime, erecting a busy civilization on a beautiful earth; and that earth is whirling through space, amid great golden worlds: and

yet, being grandsons of slime, we forget to look around us.

As Patmore expressed it:

"An idle poet, here and there,
　　Looks round him; but, for all the rest,

The world, unfathomably fair,
  Is duller than a witling's jest.
Love wakes men, once a lifetime each;
  They lift their heavy lids, and look;
And, lo, what one sweet page can teach,
  They read with joy, then shut the book."

HUMPTY-DUMPTY AND ADAM

It is not only every country that has its own language. It is each generation. The books and family letters of our grandfathers are not quite in our dialect. And so of the books of their grandfathers, and the letters they wrote. These dialects are not so different from ours that we can't make them out: they sound a little queer, that is all. Just as our own way of talking and writing (and thinking) will seem so quaint to our descendants that they'll put us away on the shelves.

A few books are written in a tongue that all times understand.

A few of us are linguists and have learned to enjoy the books of all ages.

For the rest, agèd books need translation into the speech of the day.

The poets of each generation seldom sing a new song. They turn to themes men always have loved, and sing them in the mode of their times. Each new tribe of artists perpetually repaints the same pictures. The story-men tell the same stories. They remain fresh and young.

The form is new sometimes, but never the story behind it. A few generations ago, when some one wrote Humpty-Dumpty, he was merely retelling an old story for the men of his era, one of the oldest of stories, the first part of Genesis.

It is a condensed account—it leaves out the serpent and Eve and the apple. Some editor blue-penciled these parts, perhaps, as fanciful little digressions. "Stick to the main theme," said the editor, "don't go wandering off into frills. Your story is about the fall of Adam. Get on. Make him fall."

"I had intended to introduce a love-interest," the author of Humpty-Dumpty explained.

"A love-interest!" sneered the editor. "You should have waited to be born in the twentieth century. These are manlier times. Give us men and adventure and fate."

"And what about the garden," the author sighed. "Must that be cut too?"

"By all means. Change the garden. It's a pretty enough idea in romance. But a realist who has worked in one, knows that a garden's no paradise. Genesis got it just wrong. Adam should have been exiled from town as a punishment, and put to slave in a garden."

"But town isn't paradise either. We've got to start him in paradise."

"Dear me," said the editor. "There's only one place left to put the fellow, and that's on the wall. 'Adam sat on a wall.' Begin that way."

"I'm calling him Humpty-Dumpty," the author said. "It makes it less tragic. It suggests that the fall didn't hurt Man so much after all."

"Which is true," said the editor.

I wish I had known that author. He had a kind heart. He has changed even the unforgiving cherubim in the Genesis story to those King's men who try in such a friendly way to restore Humpty-Dumpty. But the story can't let them. That would

Cinderella

leave the hero back on his wall again—like some Greek philosopher. This other way, we think of him as starting out to conquer the world.

Humpty-Dumpty and Adam

Humpty-Dumpty is a story for boys. Cinderella for girls. In Cinderella five able females, two old and three young, contend most resourcefully to capture one stupid young man. It is a terrible story. The beautiful surface barely masks the hungry wiles underneath. But it's true. It depicts the exact situation a marrying girl has to face; and, even while she's a tot in the nursery, it reminds her to plan.

But these are examples of stories that live, and last for more than one age. The mortality is heavier in other fields. For instance, philosophy. Great philosophical works of past eras are still alive in a sense, but they dwell among us as foreigners do, while Mother Goose has been naturalized.

Modern philosophies are so different. Not many centuries ago, in those eras when few changes took place, men thought of the world as something to study, instead of to mold. It was something to appropriate and possess, to be sure, but not to transform.

Humpty-Dumpty sat on the wall, then. He hadn't begun his new life.

There were few inventors in those old times, and few of those few were honored. Edison among the Greeks would have been as lonely as Plato with us.

Civilization was Thought. It was measured by

what men knew and felt of eternal things. It was wisdom.

Civilization today is invention: it is measured by our control over nature. If you remind a modern that nature is not wholly ductile, he is profoundly discouraged! "We *expect* to make over and control our world." We not only assume it is possible, we assume it is best.

Will and Wisdom are both mighty leaders. Our times worship Will.

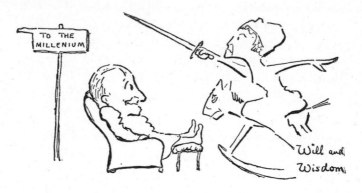

Will and Wisdom

SIC SEMPER DISSENTERS

Written during the war-time censorship of President Woodrow Wilson's Postmaster-General.

In the town of Hottentottenville an aged Hottentot,
 Whose name was Hottentotten-tillypoo,
Was slowly hottentottering around a vacant lot,
 With a vacant look upon his higaboo.
Now higaboo is Hottentot, as you may know, for face,
And to wear a vacant look upon your face is a disgrace.
But poor old Mr. Tillypoo, he had no other place—
 Though I understand it grieved him through and
  thru.

He was grubbing up potatoes in an aimless sort of way,
 Which really was the only way he had,
And an officer was watching him to see what he would
  say,
 And arrest him if the things he said were bad.
For it seems this wretched Tillypoo had gone and had
  the thought
That his neighbors didn't always do exactly as they
  ought;
And as this was rank sedition, why, they hoped to see
  him caught,
 For it naturally made them pretty mad,

So the men of Hottentottenville, they passed a little
    law,
  Which they called the Hotta-Shotta-Shootum Act,
Which fixed it so the postman was a sort of Grand
    Bashaw,
  Who determined what was false and what was fact.
And the postman sentenced Tillypoo, and wouldn't
    hear his wails,
But gave him twenty years apiece in all the local jails,
And said he couldn't vote no more, and barred him
    from the mails,
  And expressed the hope that this would teach him
    tact.

Well, the last I heard of Tilly he was planning not to
    think,
  And he'd tied a piece of string around his tongue,
And he never went within a mile of either pen or ink,
  And he always stood when *any* song was sung.
And maybe you are thinking that his fate was rather
    tough,
But what I say is, not a bit, they didn't do enough.
When anybody differs with you, dammit, treat 'em
    rough,
  Why, they ought to be bub-boiled alive and hung!

HOMES IN THE ARCTIC

No place in the world looks more hostile to man than the Arctic. The jungle arouses fear too, but it is bursting with life, and even a stranger who gets lost in it doesn't at first lose all hope. He knows he must look out for its hidden and poisonous foes, but at the thought of any such perils a man grows alert. In the Arctic, alertness seems useless. All is desolate. Dead.

Yet men are such enterprising beings, so ingenious and brave, that ages ago they learned how to live there. They settled down in the drear North, they married and brought up their babies. They made it their home.

Men of our race do not think of the Arctic as a possible home. They have gone north to find the Pole, but only as a spectacular deed. In other regions foreigners who come to visit send for their families and settle down as naturalized citizens. Not in the Arctic.

Rasmussen, who died not so long ago, was a Greenlander Dane, who didn't share our rather child-like interest in reaching the Pole, but who

did love the Northland and want to know the
Eskimo tribesmen. He learned their language and
some of their customs before he went to the Arctic,
and at his very first encounter with any of them
he was ready to meet them as friends.

He was driving his sledge across the cold, silent
whiteness, on his very first journey, when far away
he heard a shot. He thought for a moment it might
have come from his party behind. But no, it was
from in front. Three or four miles away, he saw a
line of tiny black objects in that empty land. They
looked like small reefs of bare rock standing out
from the snow.

He got out his glass and saw that they were a
line of dog-teams and sledges, which had stopped
to watch this intruder coming up from the South.
Were they shooting at him or merely warning him
that he must halt?

One man detached himself from the distant
party and came running toward Rasmussen, his
harpoon in his hand. Rasmussen didn't stop to
think whether or not this was a threat. That running harpooner and his comrades were the men he
had gone North to meet. He sprang on his sledge
and urged his dogs forward.

The Eskimo was a tall, powerful man. He was
bounding straight toward Rasmussen. When they
drew near each other, Rasmussen's dogs leaped,

snapping, at him. Rasmussen jumped off his sledge, strode among them, ordering them to stand back, and without hesitation embraced the stranger in Eskimo fashion.

Breathless from his run, the big man gasped and smiled, showing his large gleaming teeth. He was one of the Akilinermiut, he said—the "men from behind the Great Sea."

His comrades came up. They were moving to their autumn camp, taking all their worldly goods with them, but to celebrate meeting this new friend they interrupted their journey.

Looking around they saw some big snowdrifts. An excellent place to build huts, they said, and settle down right where they were—in that frozen waste. Rasmussen didn't see how they could possibly build huts of loose snow, but the Eskimos laughed and said that firm snow or ice wasn't necessary. One of them made a few cuts in a drift, sliced out blocks of snow, and laid them in place, working far more dexterously and quickly than our city bricklayers. And a woman kept strewing fine snow over the walls, as they rose, thus making them thoroughly weather-proof against any gale.

As soon as the igloos were ready to live in, everyone went indoors. Blubber lamps were lit. The huts became warm. Meat was put on to boil. And these jolly human beings sat down in all that bleak desolation, and not only made themselves at home in it, but peaceful and cozy.

ODD COUNTRIES

When I went away for a vacation, which I don't any more, I was appalled at the ridiculous inconveniences of it. I have sometimes gone to the Great Mother, Nature; sometimes to hotels. Well, the Great Mother is kind, it is said, to the birds and the beasts, the small furry creatures, and even, of old, to the Indian. But I am no Indian; I am not even a small furry creature. I disliked the Great Mother. She was damp; and far too full of insects.

And as for hotels, the man in the next room always snored. And by the time that I got used to this, and got in with some gang, my vacation was over and I had to turn around and go home.

I can get more for my money by far from a book. For example, the Oppenheim novels: there are a great many of them, and to read them is almost like going on a series of tours. A man and his whole family could take six for the price of one pair of boots. Instead of trying to find some miserable mosquitoey hotel at the seashore or an old farmer's farmhouse where the old farmer will hate me on sight, and instead of packing a trunk and running errands and catching a train I go to a book-shop and buy an Oppenheim novel. When I go on a tour with him, I start off so quickly and

The farmer who hates you on sight

easily. I sit in my armchair, I turn to the first page, and it's like having a taxi at the door—"Here's your car, sir, all ready!" The minute I read that first page I am off like a shot, into a world where things never stop happening. Magnificent things! It's about as swift a change as I could ask from jog-trot daily life.

On page two, I suddenly discover that beautiful women surround me. Are they adventuresses? I cannot tell. I must beware every minute. Everybody is wary and suave, and they are all princes and diplomats. The atmosphere is heavy with the clashing of powerful wills. Paid murderers and spies are about. Hah! am I being watched? The excitement soon gets to a point where it goes to my head. I find myself muttering thickly or biting my lips—two things I never do ordinarily and should not think of doing. I may even give a hoarse cry of rage as I sit in my armchair. But I'm not in my armchair. I am on a terrace, alone, in the moonlight. A beautiful woman (a reliable one) comes swiftly toward me. Either she is enormously rich or else I am, but we don't think of

Is she an adventuress?

that. We embrace each other. Hark! There is the duke, busily muttering thickly. How am I to reply to him? I decide to give him a hoarse cry of rage. He bites his lips at me. Someone else shoots us both. All is over.

If anyone is too restless to take his vacation in books, the quaintest and queerest of countries is just round the corner. An immigrant is only allowed to stay from 8.15 to 11 p. m., but an hour in this country does more for you than a week in the mountains. No canned fish and vegetables, no babies—

I wonder, by the way, why most babies find existence so miserable? Convicts working on roadways, stout ladies in tight shoes and corsets, teachers of the French language—none of these suffer-

ing souls wail in public; *they* don't go around
with puckered-up faces, distorted and screaming,
and beating the air with clenched fists. Then why
babies? You may say it's the nurse; but look at
the patients in hospitals. They put up not only
with illness, but nurses besides. No, babies are unreasonable; they expect far too much of existence.
Each new generation that comes takes one look at
the world, thinks wildly, "Is *this* all they've done
to it?" and bursts into tears. "You might have got
the place ready for us," they would say, only they
can't speak the language. "What *have* you been

Babies seem so dissatisfied

doing all these thousands of years on this planet?
It's messy, it's badly policed, badly laid out and
built—"

Yes, Baby. It's dreadful. I don't know why we
haven't done better. I said just now that you were

unreasonable, but I take it all back. Statesmen complain if their servants fail to keep rooms and kitchens in order, but are statesmen themselves any good at getting the world tidied up? No, we none of us are. We all find it a wearisome business.

Let us go to that country I spoke of, the one round the corner. We stroll through its entrance, and we're in Theatrical-Land.

A remarkable country. May God bless the man who invented it. I always am struck by its ways, it's so odd and delightful— .

"But," someone objects (it is possible), "it isn't real."

Ah, my dear sir, what world, then, *is* real, as a matter of fact? You won't deny that it's not only children who live in a world of their own, but débutantes, college boys, business men—certainly business men, so absorbed in their game that they lose sight of other realities. In fact, there is no one who doesn't lose sight of some, is there? Well, that's all that the average play does. It drops just a few out. To be sure, when it does that, it shows us an incomplete world, and hence not the real one; but that is all that most men can bear. We spend our lives moving from one incomplete world to another, from our homes to our clubs or our offices, laughing or grumbling, talking rapidly, reading the paper, and not doing much thinking outside of our grooves. Daily life is more comfortable, somehow, if you narrow your vision. When you try to take in all the realities, all the far-away high ones, you must first become quite still and lonely. And then in your loneliness a fire begins to creep through your veins. It's—well—I don't know much about it. Shall we return to the theater?

In Belgium?

The oddest of all entertainments is a musical comedy. I remember that during the war we had one about Belgium. When the curtain went up, soldiers were talking by the light of a lantern, and clapping each other on the shoulder when their feelings grew deep. They exchanged many well-worded thoughts on their deep feelings, too, and they spoke these thoughts briskly and readily, for it was the eve of a battle. One of the soldiers blinked his eye now and then. He was taking it hard. He said briskly he probably would never see his mother again.

His comrade, being affected by this, clapped his friend on the shoulder, and said, Oh yes he would, and cheer up.

The other looked at him, stepped forward (with his chest well expanded), and said ringingly: "I was not thinking of myself, Jean. I was thinking of Bel-jum."

Songs of home

It was a trifle confusing, but we applauded him roundly for this. The light from the balcony shone full on the young hero's face. You could see he was ready for the enemy—his dark-rouged

cheeks, his penciled eyebrows proved it. He offered to sing us a song, on the subject of home.
His comrade hurried forward and clapped him
some more on the shoulder.

The orchestra started.

> *"Muth-aw,*
> *"Muth-aw,"*

roared the hero, standing stiffly at attention,

> *"Let your arms en-fo-o-ho-old me."*

All was silent on the firing-line—except of
course, for this singing. The enemy waited po-
litely. The orchestra played on. Then the song
ended, and promptly the banging of guns was
heard in the distance—and a rather mild bang hit
the shed and the lantern went out.

The audience was left there to shudder alone,
in the darkness, not knowing whether the hero
was dead—though, of course, we had hopes. . . .
Then up went the curtain, and there he stood by
a château, where a plump Belgian maid, dressed
in white silk, was pouring high tea.

An American war-correspondent appeared on
the scene. He was the humorous character of the
performance. He was always in trouble over his
passports. He had with him a Red Cross nurse
who capered about, singing songs, as did also eight
Belgian girls, from the neighboring farms. Belgian girls are all young and tuneful, the audience

learned, and they spend their time during wars dancing with war-correspondents. They wear fresh, pretty clothes. So do soldiers who come home on leave. Sky-blue uniforms, gilt, shiny boots. All was smiling in Bel-jum.

Then the clock struck eleven. The curtain went down, like a wall. We were turned out, like poor Cinderella, into the cold, noisy streets. Dense pushing crowds. Newsboys shouting, "Great Slaughter in Flanders." The wails of some baby attempting to get used to existence.

THE ANCIENT WAY

"Accept, O God," said Abraham,
"My son instead of ram or lamb.
At Thy command I've brought my knife
To sacrifice young Isaac's life."
God smiled. " 'Tis well, good Abraham!
But this time I will take the ram."

The *Ancient* Way

In many a kindlier era since,
This tale has made boys' fathers wince . . .
   Yet when the God of War feels gory,
Even today, do fathers falter?
   No—like old Abraham in the story
They lay their sons upon the altar.

LEGS VS. ARCHITECTS

I don't know how many persons who hate climbing there are in the world; there must be, by and large, a great number. I'm one, I know that. But whenever a building is erected for the use of the public, the convenience of a non-climbing person is wholly ignored.

I refer, of course, to the debonair habit which architects have of never designing an entrance that is easy to enter. Instead of leaving the entrance on the street level so that a man can walk in, they perch it on a flight of steps, so that no one can get in without climbing.

The architect's defense is, it looks better. Looks better to whom? To architects, and possibly to tourists who never go in the building. It doesn't look better to the old or the lame, I can tell you; nor to people who are tired and have enough to do without climbing steps.

There are eminent scholars in universities whose strength is taxed daily because they must daily climb a parapet to get to their studies.

Everywhere there are thousands of men and

women who must work for a living where some nonchalant architect has needlessly made their work harder.

I admit there is a dignity and beauty in a long flight of steps. Let them be used, then, around statues and monuments, where we don't have to mount them. But why put them where they add, every day, to the exertions of everyone, and bar out some of the public completely? That's a hard-hearted beauty.

Suppose that, in the eye of an architect, it made buildings more beautiful to erect them on poles, as the lake dwellers did, ages back. (It would be only a little more obsolete than putting them on top of high steps.) Would the public meekly submit to this standard and shinny up poles all their lives?

Let us take the situation of a citizen who is not a mountaineering enthusiast. He can command every modern convenience in most of his ways. But if he happens to need a book in the Public Library what does he find? He finds that some architect has built the thing like a Greek temple. It is mounted on a long flight of steps, because the Greeks were all athletes. He tries the nearest university library. It has a flight that's still longer. He says to himself (at least I do), "Very well, then, I'll buy the damn book." He goes to the book-stores. They haven't it. It is out of stock, out of print. The only available copies are those in the libraries, where they are supposed to be ready for everyone's use; and would be, too, but for the architects and their effete barricades.

This very thing happened to me last winter. I needed a book. As I was unable to climb into the Public Library, I asked one of my friends to go. He was a young man whose legs had not yet been worn out and ruined by architects. He reported that the book I wanted was on the reference shelves, and could not be taken out. If I could get in, I could read it all I wanted to, but not even the angels could bring it outside to me.

We went down there and took a look at the rampart which would have to be mounted. That high wall of steps! I tried with his assistance to climb them, but had to give up.

He said there was a side entrance. We went there, but there, too, we found steps.

"After you once get inside, there is an elevator," the doorkeeper said.

Isn't that just like an architect! To make everything inside as perfect as possible, and then keep you out!

There's a legend that a lame man once tried to get in the back way. There are no steps there, hence pedestrians are not admitted. It's a delivery entrance for trucks. So this man had himself delivered there in a packing case, disguised as the Memoirs of Josephine, and let them haul him all the way upstairs before he revealed he was not. But it seems they turn those cases upside down and every which way in handling them, and he had to be taken to the hospital. He said it was like going over Niagara.

If there must be a test imposed on everyone who enters a library, have a brain test, and keep out all readers who are weak in the head. No matter how good their legs are, if their brains aren't first-rate, keep 'em out. But, instead, we impose a leg test, every day of the year, on all comers. We let in the brainless without any examination at all, and shut out the most scholarly persons unless they have legs like an antelope's.

If an explorer told us of some tribe that did this, we'd smile at their ways, and think they had something to learn before they could call themselves civilized.

There are especially lofty steps built around the Metropolitan Museum, which either repel or tire out visitors before they get in. Of those who do finally arrive at the doors, up on top, many never have enough strength left to view the exhibits. They just rest in the vestibule awhile, and go home, and collapse.

Legs vs. Architects

It is the same way with most of our churches, and half of our clubs. Why, they are even beginning to build steps in front of our great railway stations. Yes, that is what happens when railway men trust a "good" architect. He designs something that will make it more difficult for people to travel, and will discourage them and turn them back if possible at the start of their journey. And all this is done in the name of art. Why can't art be more practical?

There's one possible remedy:

No architect who had trouble with his own legs would be so inconsiderate. His trouble is, unfortunately, at the other end. Very well, break his legs. Whenever we citizens engage a new architect to put up a building, let it be stipulated in the contract that the Board of Aldermen shall break his legs first. The only objection I can think of is that his legs would soon get well. In that case, elect some more aldermen and break them again.

ON COWS

I was thinking the other evening of cows. You say Why? I can't tell you. But it came to me, all of a sudden, that cows lead hard lives. It takes such a lot of grass, apparently, to keep a cow going that she has to spend all her time eating, day in and day out. Dogs bounce around and bark, horses caper, birds fly, also sing, while the cow looks on, enviously, maybe, unable to join them. Cows may long for conversation or prancing, for all that we know, but they can't spare the time. The problem of nourishment takes every hour: a pause might be fatal. So they go through life drearily eating, resentful and dumb. Their food is most uninteresting, and is frequently covered with bugs; and their thoughts, if they dwell on their hopeless careers, must be bitter.

In the old days, when huge and strange animals roamed through the world, there was an era when great size was necessary, as a protection. All creatures that could do so grew large. It was only thus they felt safe. But as soon as they became large, the grass-eating creatures began to have trouble, because of the fact that grass has a low nutritive value. You take a dinosaur, for instance, who was

If cows had time —

sixty or seventy feet long. Imagine what a hard task it must have been for him, every day, to get enough grass down his throat to supply his vast body. Do you wonder that, as scientists tell us, they died of exhaustion? Some starved to death even while feverishly chewing their cud--the remoter parts of their bodies fainting from famine while their fore-parts got fed.

This imminent fate is what darkens the life of the cow.

SEX, RELIGION AND BUSINESS

A young Russian once, in the old nineteenth-century days, revisited the town he was born in, and took a look at the people. They seemed stupid —especially the better classes. They had narrow-minded ideas of what was proper and what wasn't. They thought it wasn't proper to love, except in one prescribed way. They worried about money, and social position and customs. The young Russian was sorry for them; he felt they were wasting their lives. His own way of regarding the earth was as a storehouse of treasures—sun, air, great thoughts, great experiences, work, friendship and love. And life was our one priceless chance to delight in all this. I don't say he didn't see much more to life than enjoyment, but he did believe in living richly, and not starving himself.

The people he met, though, were starving themselves all the time. Certain joys that their natures desired they would not let themselves have, be cause they had got in the habit of thinking them wrong.

Well, of course this situation is universal; it's everywhere. Most men and women have social and moral ideas which result in their starving their natures. If they should, well and good. But if not, it is a serious and ridiculous matter. It's especially hard upon those who don't see what they are doing.

I know in my own case that I have been starved, more than once. I'm not starved at the moment; but I'm not getting all I want either. So far as the great joys of life go, I live on a diet. And when something reminds me what splendors there may be, round the corner, I take a look out of the door and begin to feel restless. I dream I see life passing by, and I reach for my hat.

But a man like myself doesn't usually go at all far. His code is too strong—or his habits. Something keeps the door locked. Most of us are that way; we aren't half as free as we seem. When a man has put himself into prison it is hard to get out.

To go back to this Russian, he was in a novel of Artzibashef's, called *Sanine*. I thought at first that he might release me from my little jail. But it is an odd thing: we victims get particular about being freed. We're unwilling to be released by just anyone: it must be the right man. It's too bad to look a savior in the mouth, but it is highly important. This man Sanine, for instance, was for letting me out the wrong door.

I didn't see this at the start. In fact I felt drawn to him. I liked his being silent and caustic and strong in his views. The only thing was, he kept getting a little off-key. There was a mixture of wrongness in his rightness that made me distrust him.

Sanine was in his twenties, and in order to get all the richness that his nature desired, he had to attend to his urgent sexual needs. He wasn't in love, but his sexual needs had to be gratified. In arranging for this he recognized few or no moral restrictions. His idea was that people were apt to make an awful mistake when they tried to build permanent relations out of these fleeting pleasures. Even if there were babies.

These views didn't commend themselves to some of Sanine's neighbors and friends, or to that narrow village. They believed in family-life, and in marrying, and all that kind of thing, and they got no fun at all out of having illegitimate children. They had a lot of prejudices, those people. Sanine gave them a chill. Among them was a young man named Yourii; he's the villain of this book. He was not wicked, but stupid, poor fellow. He was pure and proud of it. I hardly need state that he came to a very bad end. And when they urged

Sanine, who was standing there at Yourii's burial, to make some little speech, he replied: "What is there to say? One fool less in the world." This made several people indignant, and the funeral broke up.

A friend of Sanine's named Ivanoff went with

He was pure and proud of it

him to the country one day, and they passed some girls bathing in a stream there, without any bathing-suits.

"Let's go and look at them," suggested Sanine.

"They would see us."

"No they wouldn't. We could land there, and go through the reeds."

"Leave them alone," said Ivanoff, blushing

slightly. . . . "They're girls . . . young ladies. . . . I don't think it's quite proper."

"You're a silly fool," laughed Sanine. "Do you mean to say that you wouldn't like to see them? What man wouldn't do the same if he had the chance?"

"Yes, but if you reason like that, you ought to watch them openly. Why hide yourself?"

"Because it's much more exciting."

"I dare say, but I advise you not to—"

"For chastity's sake, I suppose?"

"If you like."

"But chastity is the very thing that we don't possess."

Ivanoff smiled, and shrugged his shoulders.

"Look here, my boy," said Sanine, steering toward the bank, "if the sight of girls bathing were to rouse in you no carnal desire, then you would have the right to be called chaste. Indeed though I should be the last to imitate it, such chastity on your part would win my admiration. But, having these natural desires, if you attempt to suppress them, then I say that your so-called chastity is all humbug."

This was one of the incidents that made me dislike Mr. Sanine. I liked his being honest, and I liked his being down on prudery and humbug. But I thought his theory of life was a good deal too simple. "Don't repress your instincts," he said. That's all very well, but suppose a man has more than one kind? If a cheap peeping instinct says "Look," and another instinct says "Oh, you bounder," which will you suppress? It comes down to a question of values. Life holds moments for most of us which the having been a bounder will spoil.

The harmonizing of body and spirit and all the instincts into one, so we'll have no conflicting desires, is an excellent thing—when we do it; and we can all do it some of the time, with the will and the brains to. But no one can all the time. And when you are not fully harmonized, and hence feel a conflict—different parts of your nature desiring to go different ways—why, what can you do? You must just take your choice of repressions.

As to Sanine, his life is worth reading, and—in spots—imitating. But I thought he was rather a cabbage. A cabbage is a strong, healthy vegetable, honest and vigorous. It's closely in touch with nature, and it doesn't pretend to be what it isn't. You might do well to study a cabbage: but not follow its program. A cabbage has too much to learn. How our downright young moderns will learn things, I'm sure I don't know. Sanine scornfully says "not by repression." Well, I don't think highly of repressions; they're not the best method.

Yet it's possible that they might be just the thing—for a cabbage.

Long before Sanine was born—in the year 1440 in fact—there was a man in India who used to write religious little songs. Name of Kabir. I tried to read his books once, but couldn't, not liking extremes. He was pretty ecstatic. I could no more

I couldn't keep up with Kabir

keep up with him than with Sanine.

In his private life Kabir was a married man and had several children. By trade he was a weaver. Weaving's like knitting: it allows you to make a living and think of something else at the same time. It was the very thing for Kabir, of course. Gave him practically the whole day to make songs in, and think of religion. He seems to have been a happy fellow—far more so than Sanine.

Sanine's comment would have been that Kabir was living in an imaginary world, not a real one, and that he was autointoxicating himself with his dreamings.

Kabir's answer would have been that Sanine ought to try that world before judging it, and had better begin by just loving people a little. More love, and more willingness to deal with his poor fellow-creatures, instead of flinging them off in impatience—that would have been Kabir's prescription. And, as a fact, it might really have been an eye-opener for Sanine.

Of the two, however, I preferred Sanine to Kabir. The trouble with Kabir was, he wouldn't let you alone. He wanted everybody to be as religious as he was: it would make them so happy, he thought. This made him rather screechy.

He sang some songs, however, that moved me. Like many a modern, I'm not religious; that is,

I've no creed; but I don't feel quite positive that this army of planets just happened, and that man's evolution from blindness to thought was an accident and that nowhere is any Intelligence vaster than mine.

Therefore, I'm always hoping to win some real spiritual insight. It has come to other men without dogma (I can't accept dogmas) and so, I keep thinking, it may some day come to me, too. I never really expect it next week, though. It's always far off. It might come, for instance, I think, in the hour of death. And here is the song Kabir sang to all men who think that:

> *"O Friend! hope for Him whilst you live, know whilst you live, understand whilst you live; for in life deliverance abides.*
>
> *"If your bonds be not broken whilst living, what hope of deliverance in death?*
>
> *"It is but an empty dream, that the soul shall have union with Him because it has passed from the body:*
>
> *"If He is found now, He is found then.*
>
> *"If not, we do but go to dwell in the City of Death.*
>
> *"If you have union now, you shall have it hereafter."*

Both Sanine and Kabir should have read

Tarkington's novel, *The Turmoil,* which is all about the rush and hustle-bustle of life in America. It would have made them see what great contrasts exist in this world. Kabir thought too much about religion. Sanine, of sex. Nobody in *The Turmoil* was especially troubled with either. Some went to church, maybe, and sprinkled a little religion here and there on their lives; but none deeply felt it, or woke up in the morning thinking about it, or allowed it to have much say when they made their decisions. And as to sex, though there were lovers among them, it was only incidentally that they cared about that. They satisfied nature in a routine way, outside office hours. No special excitement about it. Nothing hectic—or magical.

Now, sex is a fundamental state and concern of existence: it's a primary matter. If it's pushed to one side, we at least should be careful what does it. And religion, too, God or no God, is a primary matter, if we stretch the word to cover all the spiritual gropings of man. Yet what is it that pushes these two great things aside in America? What makes them subordinate? Business. We put business first.

And what is this business? What is the charm of this giant who engrosses us so? In Tarkington's novel you find yourself in a town of neighborly people, in the Middle West somewhere; a leisurely and kindly place—home-like, it used to be called. But in the hearts of these people was implanted a longing for size. They wished that town to grow. So it did. (We can all have our wishes.) And with its new bigness came an era of machinery and rush. "The streets began to roar and rattle, the houses to tremble, the pavements were worn under the tread of hurrying multitudes. The old, leisurely, quizzical look of the faces was lost in something harder and warier."

"You don't know what it means, keepin' property together these days," says one of them. "I tell you when a man dies the wolves come out of the woods, pack after pack . . . and if that dead man's children ain't on the job, night and day, everything he built'll get carried off. . . . My Lord! when I think of such things coming to *me*! It don't seem like I deserved it—no man ever tried harder to raise his boys right than I have. I planned and planned and planned how to bring 'em up to be guards to drive the wolves off, and how to be builders to build, and build bigger. . . . What's the use of my havin' worked my life and soul into my business, if it's all goin' to be dispersed and scattered, soon as I'm in the ground?"

Poor old business! It does look pretty sordid. Yet there is a soul in this giant. Consider its power to call forth the keenness in men and to give endless zest to their toil and sharp trials to their courage. It is grimy, shortsighted, this master—but it has greatness, too.

Only, as we all know, it does push so much else to one side! Love, spiritual gropings, the arts, our old closeness to nature, the independent outlook and disinterested friendships of men—all these must be checked and diminished, lest they interfere. Yet those things are life; and big business is just a great game. Why play any game so intently we forget about life?

Well, looking around at mankind, we see some races don't. Others, especially the white races, play their games hard. Knight-errantry was once the game. See how hard they played that. The Crusades, too,—all gentlemen were supposed to take in the Crusades. Old, burly, beef-crunching wine-bibbers climbed up on their chargers and went through incredible troubles and dangers—for what? Why, to rescue a shrine, off in Palestine, from the people who lived there. Those people, the Saracens, weren't doing anything very much to it; but still it was thought that no gentleman ought to stay home, or live his life normally, until that bit of land had been rescued, and put in the hands of business-like prelates instead of those Saracens.

Sex, Religion and Business

Men once made a business of exploring new lands and new worlds. Cortez, Frobisher, Drake. Imagine a dialogue in those days between father and son, a sea-going father who thought exploration was life, and a son who was weakly and didn't want to be forced into business. "I don't like exploration much, Father. I'm seasick the whole time, you know; and I can't bear this going ashore and oppressing the blacks." "Nonsense, boy! This work's got to be done. It'll make a man of you."

THE MAN WHO KNEW GODS

His case illustrated the risks explorers run. Not the physical risks, which are overestimated, but the psychological dangers. For years he had lived among savages, observing their ways, and owing to this he had fallen into a completely detached mental habit. When he returned to civilization, he had become a confirmed looker-on. He couldn't get back into touch with us. He remained an outsider.

I met him but once myself. I was in the publishing business at the time, and, hearing that this man was in New York, I thought I might as well see him about his next book. Telephoning him, therefore, at his hotel, I asked him to dine with me on the following Friday.

"Fri-day?" he replied. "What is 'Friday'?" (He spoke English perfectly.)

"It is the twenty-sixth," I answered.

He said: "The twenty-sixth what? Oh, I know," he continued; "Friday is a day of the week. Thank you very much, but I do not keep track of my dinners so carefully as that."

This rather odd answer I passed over, at the moment, thinking I had misunderstood him; and we arranged that he would come some day to my office instead, after lunch.

The next that I heard, he had called there at a quarter to five, the hour at which I always leave. My secretary explained to him that I had gone.

He looked at my desk, on which lay some unfinished business, and said to my secretary, "Why?"

The man courteously responded, "Because it is a quarter to five."

The explorer thereat laughed weirdly and went off.

I now perceived I had to deal with a most eccentric character; but that being a necessary evil in the publishing business, I went to his hotel at nine o'clock that evening. I found him down in the restaurant eating oatmeal and succotash, and we then and there had the following extravagant interview,—which I give without comment.

"The book *I* mean to write," he said, staring at me, "is a study of actual religions. Other writers have told the world what men of all countries suppose their religions to be. I shall tell what they really are."

I said that our house would prefer an account of his travels; but he paid no attention.

"Men's real religions," he announced, "are unknown to themselves. You may have heard of the Waam Islanders," he leisurely continued. "They, for instance, would tell you that their deity was an idol called Bashwa, a large crumbling stone thing which stands in a copperwood forest. They worship this idol most faithfully, on the first of each lunar month. No Waam Islander would ever acknowledge he had any other god but Bashwa.

"But a stranger soon notices that in every hut and cave in that country, hanging beside the water-jar, is a long sleeping-mat, and on that mat a rough pattern is drawn, like a face. 'What is that?' I asked them. 'That? oh, that's G'il,' they answered in an off-hand careless way, without any of the reverence they would have used if they had thought G'il a god. But nevertheless I noted that everywhere, throughout that whole island, submissive remarks about G'il were far more numerous than those about Bashwa. That made me begin collecting those references; and presently I found that most things of which that tribe approved were spoken of as being g'il, or very g'il, and things they didn't like were damned as na-g'il.

"It was a little difficult to understand their exact conception of G'il, but apparently it typified the hut, or the hut point of view. Marriage was g'il, and good manners and building materials, because they all made for hut-life. Inhospitality was na-g'il, and the infidelity of women, and earthquakes, and leaks.

"They sometimes personified G'il and talked of him as he. 'G'il loves not Wheesha' (the wind); 'G'il comforts the weary'; 'G'il says, "Get more children." ' But all this was only in their fanciful moments. At other times G'il was merely the mat that they slept on. When I said to them, 'G'il is your real God,' they laughed at my stupidity—good-humoredly, as though there were something, perhaps, in my idea, yet with a complacent assurance that I was preposterous. I did not argue with them. One couldn't, you know. I simply continued my observations, corroborating my theory at every turn. To give you an instance: Bashwa is supposed to think highly of hunters and sailors, and the Waam-folk always profess to think highly of them too. That attitude, however, is only official, not real. Very few of them actually become sailors. The life is na-g'il."

He came to a pause.

"I wonder whether we, too, have a G'il," I said, to humor him. "We shall have to ask some of your Waam-folk to come here and tell us."

The explorer looked me over as though he were "continuing his observations" of *my* manners and customs. "Yes," he said, "there's a white man's G'il."

I regretted having mentioned it.

"Can't you guess what he is?" he inquired. "I say 'he' because, like the Waam G'il, he is sometimes personified. Come now! Apply the test. He doesn't typify the Waam Islander point of view: he isn't a mat. But examine your huts and your conversation, and you'll easily spot him. No, I'm not talking of money, or power, or success: you may bow down to these,—but not blindly. You at least know what you are doing. The worship of a G'il is unconscious, and hence more insidious. Even when an explorer points it out, you won't see its importance. It will seem insignificant to you. And yet, while the Bashwa to whom you build temples is only occasionally deferred to, this G'il of yours sways you in all things. He is the first whom you think of when you rise, and the last when you go to bed. You speak of your G'il hourly or oftener, all day long. Those of you who heed him too little are disapproved of by everybody, while the American who succeeds in life is the man who is most careful of G'il.

"I have habits," he morosely continued, "of doing certain things—eating my meals, for instance —at quite different hours from those that are prevalent here. I find that everyone who hears of this is surprised at my ways. Their attitude, while not openly intolerant, is distinctly disapproving. When

I ask them why, I get no answer—no rational answer. They say simply, 'It's the wrong time.' Following up this clue I have noticed that not only is the time for performing an act supposed to be sometimes 'wrong' and sometimes 'right,' but that the idea of time governs all of you, like an absolute tyrant. Even your so-called free-thinkers, who lead a life without God, never dream of daring to live without a clock and a calendar. And just as the Waam-folk are unconsciously obsessed by their hut-thought, and see everything from that angle, so you have drifted into an exaggerated preoccupation with time. No matter what you may want to do, you first look at the clock, to see if it is the right time for doing it: if it isn't, you wait. You feel that you 'ought' to. . . . And each caste among you has its own hours. A difference of thirty minutes in the hour at which a family has dinner, marks a difference in their social scale. 'There isn't time,' you sigh, submissively, when you give up something you'd like to do. 'Time is money,' is one of your phrases. 'Give me time,' is your prayer. Your big books of maxims are full of the respect you feel toward him. 'The greatest crime is loss of time.' 'Time flies.' 'Time waits for no man.' These are only small instances, but their total effect is not small, for it is life itself that you sacrifice to this fetish. Your G'il actually won't let you take good full draughts of existence—he keeps you so busy dividing it into months, days, and minutes. You imagine that it is because you lead crowded lives that you do it. But it is because you're always thinking of time that you lead crowded lives.

"You are smiling at me good-humoredly, my friend. I see that, like the Waam Islanders, you think I am preposterous. It is the old story. You cannot view yourself from without. You will admit that considerations of time enter into all your acts, and yet—this seems trivial? And it is inconceivable to you that you are its slaves?"

"My dear sir," I interposed, "a strict observance of the laws of time enables a man to live a much fuller life."

"It is what all devotees say of all gods," he murmured.

"We are not its slaves," I continued. "That's absurd. We have only a sensible regard for it, as everyone must."

"Ah! ah!" he cried. "But you do not say 'one must' when your Bashwa speaks.

"Your Bashwa thinks highly of those who do good works without ceasing. You profess to think highly of them too; that is your official attitude. In reality, how very few of you lead that life. It happens to be na-g'il, you see. You haven't the time.

"Look about you if you would convince your-self. The concrete evidence alone is enough. On the breasts or the wrists of your women, and in every man's pocket you see a G'il amulet, a watch, to remind them of time every hour. What other god was ever so faithfully worshipped? In every hut in the land you will find his altar, and in your large huts you will find one in every principal room. No matter how free and unconventional their owners may be, no matter how those rooms may vary in their arrangement or furnishings, there stands always in the most prominent place the thing called the mantel; on it, ceremoniously flanked by two candlesticks, or vases, sits G'il, the timepiece; and his is the face of all others you most frequently consult. Blind and idolatrous tribesman! time is your deity!"

Well, that's all there was to our interview, for at this point he came to a pause and I rose to leave, explaining to him that I had to go because it was getting so late.

HOW IT LOOKS TO A FISH

✧

The most ordinary steamship agent, talking of tours around the world, can describe them in such a way that people will pack up and start off at once. But even the most gifted preachers have never been able to get men to hurry to heaven.

All sorts of prophets have dreamed of a heaven, and they have imagined all kinds; they have put houris in the Mahometan's paradise, and swords in Valhalla. But in spite of having carte blanche they have never invented a good one.

The average man sits in his pew, hearing about halos, and when it's all over he goes home and puts on his old wrapper. "I suppose I can stand it," he thinks. "I've stood corns and neuritis. But I just hate the idea of floating around any such region."

Some good persons want to go to heaven so as to keep out of hell, or to get away from misery here—if they are in great enough misery. Others think of it as a place to meet friends in, or as a suitable destination for relatives. But the general idea is it's like being cast away in the tropics: the surroundings are gorgeous, and it's pleasant and warm—but not home.

It seems too bad that heaven should always be

" I've stood corns
and neuritis—"

somehow repugnant, and unfit as it were for human habitation.

Assuming that we are immortal, what happens to a man when he dies? The spiritualists, who offer us one of the most repugnant heavens of all, say there are several stages. At first the surround-

"But I just hate
the idea of floating"

ings in the new life seem shadowy, then after a bit they grow solid; and then it is the world left behind that seems vague. You lose touch with it and with those whom you knew there—except when they think of you. When they think of you, although you can see them, and feel what they're thinking, it isn't like hearing the words that they say, or their voices; it's not like looking over their shoulders to see what they write; it's more like sensing what is in their thoughts.

But at first you are too bewildered to do this. You are in a new world, and you find yourself surrounded by spirits, telling you that you're dead. The spiritualists say that many new arrivals refuse to believe they are dead, and look around skeptically at heaven, and think they are dreaming. It often takes a long time to convince them. This must be rather awkward. It's as though no one who arrived in Chicago would believe he was there, but went stumbling around, treating citizens as though they weren't real, and saying that he doubted whether there was any such place as Chicago.

But if there was any truth in this picture, it would explain things. If the spirits themselves cannot clearly take in their new life at first, how can we possibly expect to imagine it or ever understand what it's like? And, not understanding, what wonder we don't find it attractive?

You can't describe one kind of existence to those in another.

How It Looks to a Fish

Suppose, for example, we were describing dry land to a fish.

"We have steam-heat and sunsets," I might tell him—just for a beginning.

And the fish would think: "Heat? Phew! that's murderous! And oh, that sizzling old sun!"

"We have legs," I might add.

"What are legs?"

"Things to walk on. They're like sticks, that grow right on our bodies. We do not use fins."

"What, no fins! Why, with fins, just a flicker will shoot me in any direction. Legs are clumsy and slow: think of tottering around on such stumps! And you can only go on the level with them; you can't rise and dip."

"Yes, we can. We build steps."

"But how primitive!"

Perhaps he would ask me what drawbacks there were to earthly existence; and how he would moan when I told him about bills and battles.

"And is it true," he might say, "that there really are beings called dentists? Weird creatures, who pull your poor teeth out, and hammer your mouths? Bless my gills! it sounds dreadful! Don't ask me to leave my nice ocean!"

Then, to be fair, he might ask. "What's the other side of the picture, old man? What pleasures have you that would tempt me? What do you do to

amuse yourselves?" And I would tell him about
Charlie Chaplin, and the Opera House, business,
and poetry—but how could I describe Charlie
Chaplin from the fish point of view? And poetry?
—getting ecstasy from little black dots on a page?
"You get soulful over *that* kind of doings?" he
would ask, with a smile. "Well, all right, but it
sounds pretty crazy to a sensible fish."

"Business is the main thing here, anyhow," I'd
answer.

"And what's 'business'?"

"Well, it's—er—it's like this: Suppose you, for

He smiled dreamily

instance, were to go and catch a great many flies—"

The fish would look pleased and smile dreamily.

"But then not eat them, mind you."

"Not *eat* them?"

"No, but put them all out on a bit of flat rock, for a counter, and 'sell' them to other fish: exchange them, I mean—for shells, let us say, if you used shells as money."

The fish would look puzzled. "But what *for,* my dear sir?" he'd inquire. "What would I do with shells?"

"Exchange them for flies again, see?"

"**O my soul! what a life!**"

OBJECTIONS TO READING

When I was five years old I felt I couldn't wait any longer: I wanted to read. My parents had gone along supposing that there was no hurry; and they were quite right; there wasn't. But I was impatient. I couldn't wait for people to read to me—they so often were busy, or they insisted on reading

the wrong thing, or stopping too soon. I had an immense curiosity to explore the book-universe, and the only way to do it satisfactorily was to do it myself.

Consequently I got hold of a reader, which said,

"See the Dog Run!" It added, "The Dog Can Run and Leap," and stated other obvious facts. "The Apple is Red," was one of them, I remember, and "The Round Ball Can Roll."

There was certainly nothing thrilling about the exclamation, "See the Dog Run!" Dogs ran all the time. The performance was too common to speak of. Nevertheless, it did thrill me to spell it out for myself in a book. "The Round Ball Can Roll," said my book. Well, I knew that already. But it was wonderful to have a book say it. It was having books talk to me.

Years went on, and I read more and more. Sometimes, deep in Scott, before dinner, I did not hear the bell, and had to be hunted up by someone and roused from my trance. I hardly knew where I was, when they called me. I got up from my chair not knowing whether it was for dinner or breakfast or for school in the morning. Sometimes, late at night, even after a long day of play—those violent and never-pausing exertions that we call play, in boyhood—I would still try to read, hiding the light, until my eyes closed in spite of me. So far as I knew, there were not many books in the world; but nevertheless I was in a hurry to read all there were.

In this way, I ignorantly fastened a habit upon me. I got like an alcoholic, I could let no day go

by without reading. As I grew older, I couldn't
pass a book-shop without going in. And in libraries,
where reading was free, I always read to excess.
The people around me glorified the habit (just
as old songs praise drinking). I never had the
slightest suspicion that it might be a vice. I was as
complacent over my book totals as six-bottle men
over theirs.

Can there ever have been a race of beings on
some other star so fascinated as we are by reading?
It is a remarkable appetite. It seems to me that it
must be peculiar to simians. Would you find the
old folks of any other species, with tired old brains,
feeling vexed if they didn't get a whole newspaper
fresh every morning? Back in primitive times,
when men had nothing to read but knots in a
string, or painful little pictures on birch bark—
was it the same even then? Probably Mrs. Flint-
Arrow, 'way back in the Stone Age, pored over
letters from her son, as intensely as anyone. "Only
two knots in it this time," you can almost hear her
say to her husband. "Really I think Ak might be a
little more frank with his mother. Does it mean
he has killed that striped Wumpit in Double Rock
Valley, or that the Gouly family where you told
him to visit has twins?"

There are one or two primitive ideas we still
have about reading. I remember in a boarding-

house in Tucson, I once met a young clergyman, who exemplified the belief many have in the power of books. "Here are you," he would say to me, "and here is your brain. What are you going to

a K and the striped Wumpit —

put into it? That is the question." I could make myself almost as good as a bishop, he intimated, by choosing the noblest and best books, instead of mere novels. One had only to choose the right sort of reading to be the right sort of man.

He seemed to think I had only to read Socrates to make myself wise, or G. Bernard Shaw to be witty.

Cannibals eat the hearts of dead enemy chieftains, to acquire their courage; and this clergyman entered a library with the same simple notion.

But though books are weak implements for implanting good qualities in us, they do color our minds, fill them with pictures and sometimes ideas. There are scenes of horror in my mind today that were put there by Poe, or Ambrose Bierce or somebody, years ago, which I cannot put out. No maiden in distress would bother me nowadays, I have read of too many, but some of those first ones I read of still make me feel cold. Yes, a book can leave indelible pictures. . . . And it can

maiden in distress

introduce wild ideas. Take a nice old lady for instance, at ease on her porch, and set the ballads of Villon to grinning at her over the hedge, or a deep-growling Veblen to creeping on her, right down the rail,—it's no wonder they frighten her. She doesn't want books to show her the under-world and blacken her life.

Dastardly attack by Veblen's latest

It's not surprising that some books are censored and forbidden to circulate. The surprising thing is that in this illiberal world they travel so freely. But they usually aren't taken seriously; I suppose that's the answer. It's odd. Many countries that won't admit even the quietest living man without passports will let in the most active, emancipating thoughts in a novel.

The habit of reading increases. How far can it go? The innate capacity of our species for it is plainly enormous. Are we building a race of men who will read several books every day, not counting a dozen newspapers at breakfast, and magazines

Scenes of Horror

in between? It sounds like a lot, but our own record would have astonished our ancestors. Our descendants are likely to read more and faster than we.

People used to read chiefly for knowledge or to pursue lines of thought. There wasn't so much

The underworld

fiction as now. These proportions have changed.
We read some books to feed our curiosity but more
to feed our emotions. In other words, we moderns
are substituting reading for living.

Volume of morbid Geography
attempting to enter Lone Gulch

When our ancestors felt restless they burst out
of their poor bookless homes, and roamed around
looking for adventure. We read someone else's.
The adventures our ancestors had were often un-
satisfactory, and the people they met in the course
of them were hard to put up with. We can choose
just the people and adventures we like in our
books. But our ancestors got real emotions, where
we live on canned.

Of course canned emotions are thrilling at times,
in their way, and wonderful genius has gone into
putting them up. But a man going home from a

library where he has read of some battle, has not the sensations of a soldier returning from war.

Still—for us—reading is natural. If we were more robust, as a race, or if earth-ways were kinder, we should not turn so often to books when we wanted more life. But a fragile yet aspiring species on a stormy old star—why, a substitute for living is the very thing such beings need.

AN ODE TO TRADE

"Recent changes in these thoroughfares show that
trade is rapidly crowding out vice."— *Real-estate item.*

O restless Spirit, from whose cup
　　All drink, and at whose feet all bow,
May I inquire what you are up
　　　　To now?

Insatiable, I know, your maw,
　　And ravenous of old your shrine;
But still, O trade, you ought to draw
　　　　The line.

Our health, our pride, our every breath
　　Of leisure—do not these suffice?
Ah, tell me not you're also death
　　　　On vice.

Ah, tell me not yon gilded hell
　　That has from boyhood soothed my grief
Must fall into the sere and yel-
　　　　low leaf;

That dens my wayward comrades know
　　Must also share this cruel lot:
That every haunt of sin must go
　　　　To pot.

An Ode to Trade

I who have seen your roaring marts
    Engulf our aristocracy,
Our poets, all who love the arts
        But me:

I who have watched your bounteous purse
    Seduce, I say, the world's elect—
I, in my clear and ringing verse,
        Object.

You've stripped existence to the bone;
    You see us of all else bereft;
You know quite well that vice alone
        Is left.

You claim our every thought and prayer,
    Nor do we grudge the sacrifice.
But worms will turn! You've got to spare
        Us vice.

A HOPEFUL OLD BIGAMIST

There are any number of difficulties and bumps along the roads of this world, and yet there are plenty of easy-going people who never prepare for them. They take all such things as they come. Some are buoyant, some fearless.

But within the last hundred years, large companies have been organized to go after these people, and catch them alone somewhere and give them a good thorough fright. These companies hire men who are experts at that sort of thing; men who make it their life-work to find fearless persons and scare them.

But no matter how ambitious and active these experts may be, they cannot catch every one personally. It would take too much time. So they write gloomy advertisements which are designed to scare people in general.

These advertisements are a characteristic feature of our civilization.

Man goes down-town, whistling, sunny morning. Happens to pick up a magazine. Immediately he gets hit in the eye with a harrowing picture. Sometimes it is one that reminds him he may die any minute, and depicts his widow and children limping around in the streets, hunting crusts. Or it may be a picture of his house burning up, or his motor upsetting. Or an illness, and there he is lying flat and weak on his bed.

After he has seen a good many pictures like that, he grows quiet. Stops whistling. He learns how to

worry, and he worries off and on till it hurts. Then, to get some relief, he makes a contract with one of those companies, which provides him with what we call insurance, for an annual tribute.

I hope no one will think I am disparaging insurance, which is a useful arrangement. It enables many of us to pool our risks and be protected from hardship. And the best companies nowadays handle the thing very well. They scare a person as little as possible. They just gently depress him. They inflict just enough mental torture to get him to put in his money. It is only when he is stubborn about it that they give him the cold chills.

Every century has some such institution. The Inquisition was worse.

Like insurance, it had high ideals, but peculiar methods.

Insurance men, however, are steadily improving their methods. Instead of always reminding you how awful it is not to insure, they sometimes print brighter pictures, which show how happy you will feel if you do. For instance, a picture of a postman bringing a check to your widow. Your widow is

thanking the postman, her face full of joy. Sometimes the old president of the company is shown in
the upper left corner, writing out the check personally, as soon as he hears of your death. Or
maybe they leave out the president and put in your
infant son, for good measure. He is playing in his
innocent way with his dead father's cane, and the
widow, with a speculative eye on him, is thought-
fully murmuring, "As soon as he is old enough I
must insure my little boy too."

In the days before it was possible to insure,
there was even more gloom. Light-hearted people
may have worried less, but the rest worried more.
They could save enough money for the future if
it was sufficiently distant, but not for a serious
disaster that might come too soon. This darkened
their outlook. They had no one to trust in but God.

There has always been a great deal of talk about
trusting in God, but human beings incline to be
moderate and cautious in trying it. As a rule no
one does it unless he has to.

Not even the clergy.

A few years ago a fund was formed, in the Epis-
copal Church, to pay agèd ministers pensions, so
they would never be destitute. This brought the
greatest happiness to many of them who were approaching decrepitude. Letters came in from

ministers who had worried in silence for years, with no one to trust but the Deity, whose plans might be strange. They described how they had wept with relief when this fund was established. Printed copies of these letters were mailed to all the good Christians who had contributed, to show them how much true joy and happiness their money had brought, and how thankful the clergy were to have something solid to trust, like a pension.

I wonder just what the average citizen had better trust? His money, or his own native mettle?

I should like to trust both.

But they tell me that that is impracticable. Won't work at all. I can *have* some of both, of course. Certainly. But I cannot *trust* both.

Like all other men I have my own inner fountain of strength, and it's been a faithful old thing; it has done a lot for me. It has vigor in it yet— but it isn't big and fiery, or strong. I could only have made it work abundantly if I had relied wholly on it. If I had done that, it would have probably called out my full powers. But instead I have relied partly on money, for fear my strength might desert me; and that fear has naturally had an effect on my strength. I work hard, but with less fire. Less eagerness. Progressively less. Any man who doesn't trust his spirit will find it will ebb.

And the same's true of money. Unless you are in love with your wealth, it will slip through your fingers. If you want to get a whole lot of money, worship gold all your days. You must be pretty devoted to win a jealous mistress like gold.

They are both jealous mistresses, that's the worst of it.

It is an awkward predicament.

I don't like to face this problem squarely. I don't get it settled. I keep on, like a hopeful old bigamist, in love with both mistresses: my money and my spirit or mettle.

I try to soothe each. I say to my mettle, "I care much more for you than for money: it's true that I keep money, too; but it's you that I love. You and I are one, aren't we? Very well, then. Come on. Let's be happy."

And I say to my money, "Now be faithful: for God's sake be faithful; don't slip off and desert me and leave me alone in the world." She looks jealously at me. "Alone?" she says; "how about that mettle of yours, you're so fond of?" "Ah, my dear," I say sadly, giving her an affectionate squeeze, "my mettle is no better than she should be. I don't like to talk of it. You are the one that I expect to comfort me in my dark moments; and I hope you and

I will be here together long after my mettle has gone."

There you have my ménage. It's been difficult. But I cannot complain. As a bigamist I suppose on the whole I've been fairly successful. Yet I know I'd have more money today—I think a great deal more money—if I had been more faithful to Mammon, as they call the poor creature. And similarly I might have led an heroic, ardent life with my mettle, if I had ever trusted it fully.

That's the trouble with bigamy.

TO EVERY MAN

To every man the moment comes
When earth and sky and sea
Are filled with glory at the sight
Of his predestined She.
In castle hall or humble cot
This miracle occurs,
Quite irrespective, it would seem,
Of any charms of hers.

THE DEATH OF LOGAN

☼

Cockroaches, like the Wise Men, originally lived in the East. They were at first far from hardy—wretched travelers, hating changes of climate. But when England began trading with the Orient, the cockroach grew venturesome, and began putting to sea as a stowaway. It was thus he reached England.

He settled down at first in her seaports. Remained there for years. People inland heard of him, or saw him if they went to the coast, but supposed themselves immune from his visits. Now he owns the whole island. And wherever the Englishman has journeyed, or settled, or trafficked, except perhaps on the ice-floes of Labrador, we now find the cockroach.

We all know his habits. He prefers to live in kitchens and bakeries. Eats all kinds of food. Eats shoes and the bindings of books. Also eats his own relatives. Any relative that becomes languid instead of lively is at once eaten up.

The sexes are easy to tell apart if you observe them: the males don't drag their stomachs on the ground the way the females do, and they have better wings. Their wings are not good enough to use much, but still, they have little ones.

The most surprising thing about roaches is that they live several years. Scientists say maybe five. Owing to this they get to know all of a family's ways, and can't be caught napping; they have plenty of time to study roach powders and learn to digest them. They dislike castor oil, though, and keep away from where it has been rubbed.

Cockroaches are intelligent beings. Look at Marquis's Archy. They are not like other insects, any more than dogs are like other animals. I wish some man of science and sympathy would interpret their lives. Or that some poet would do for the cockroach what Maeterlinck has done for the Bee.

If nobody else will, I shall probably have to do it myself.

Since boyhood (I shall begin) I have felt the injustice of men to the roach. Or not men, no; but women. Men are in this matter more tolerant, more live-and-let-live in their ways. But women have condemned the roach not only unheard, but unjudged. Not one of them has ever tried petting a roach to gain his affection. Not one of them has studied him or encouraged him to show his good side. Some cockroaches, for instance, are exceedingly playful and gay, but what chance have they to show this, when being stepped on, or chased with a broom? Suppose we had treated dogs this way; scared them; made fugitives of them!

No, the human race, though kind to its favorites, is cruel to others. The pale little, lovable cockroach has been given no show. If a housewife would call to her roaches as she does to her chickens, how they would come scampering! They would eat from her hand and lay eggs for her—they do now, in fact.

We should learn that blind enmity is not the attitude to take toward strangers. The cockroach has journeyed from Asia to come to our shores; and because he looked queer, like most Asiatics, he has been condemned from the start. The charges are that he is dirty and that he eats the food we leave lying around. Well, what of it? Eats our food, does he? Is that a crime? Do not birds do the same? And as to his being dirty, he isn't as dirty as dogs. One dog will bring in more dust and fleas and loose hairs in a day, than a colony, an empire, of cockroaches will in a year.

I remember what Mr. Burbank once said when we talked of this matter. Alluding to the fact that the cockroach likes to eat other roaches, he said why not breed a roach that wouldn't eat anything else? When one introduced these into the home they would first eat the old-timers, and then quietly devour each other until all were gone.

But how could a home remain bare of insects? Nature abhors such a vacuum. Some men would like to cover the whole world with porcelain tiles, and make old Mother Earth, as we know her, disappear from our view. They would sterilize and scrub the whole planet, so as to make the place sanitary. Well, I too feel that way at times: we all have finicky moments. But in my robust hours I sympathize with Nature. A hygienic kitchen is unnatural. It should be swarming with life. (The way mine is.)

I see a great deal of the roach when I visit my kitchen. His habits, to be sure, are nocturnal. But, then, so are mine. I admire his character. He is not socialistic and faithful, like the ant, for example: he is anarchistic, wild, temperamental, and fond of adventure. He is also contemplative by nature, like other philosophers. How many an evening, at midnight, when I have wanted a sandwich, I have found him and his friends standing still, lost in thought, by the sink. When I poke him up, he blinks with his antennæ and slowly makes off. On the other hand, he can run at high speed when the cook is pursuing him. And he zigzags his course most ingeniously. He uses his head.

Again and again I have tried to make a pet of the cockroach, for I believe under his natural distrust he has an affectionate nature. But some hostile servant has invariably undone my work. The only roach I succeeded in taming was hardly a pet, because he used to hide with the others half the time when he saw me, although once in a while he would come out at my call when I brought him warm tea. Poor fellow! poor Logan!—as I called him. He had a difficult life. I think he was slightly dyspeptic. Perhaps the tea was not good for him. He used to run about uttering low, nervous moans before molting; and when his time came to mate, I thought he never would find the right doe. How well I remember my thrill when he picked one at last, and when I knew that I was about to see their nuptial flight. Higher and higher they circled over the clean blue linoleum, with their short wings going so fast they fairly crackled, till the air was electric: and then, swirling over the dresser, their great moment came. Unhappily, Logan, with his usual bad luck, bumped the bread-box. The doe, with a shrill, morose whistle, went and lay on the floor; but Logan seemed too balked to pursue her. His flight was a failure.

He rapidly grew old after this, and used to keep by himself. He also got into the habit of roaming around outdoors at night. Hated to see other roaches mating by the bread-box, perhaps. As he was too big to crawl back in under the door when we shut it, he was sometimes locked out when he roamed, and had to wait until morning. This in the end caused his death. One winter evening, blocked at the door, he climbed the fire-escape and tried to get in the bathroom window. But it chanced to be shut. When I went to look at the thermometer in the morning, there he lay in the snow.

FROM NOAH TO NOW

In the days of Father Noah life was sweet—life was
    sweet.
He played the soft majubal every day.
And for centuries and centuries he never crossed the
    street,
    Much less supposed he'd ever move away.
But times grew bad and men grew bad, all up and
    down the land,
    And the soft majubal got all out of key;
And when the weather changed, besides, 'twas more
    than he could stand.
    So Father Noah he packed and put to sea.

And "Yo-ho-ho," with a mournful howl, said the poor
    old boy to Ham;
And "Yo-ho-ho," sang Japhet, and a pink but tuneful
    clam;
And "Yo-ho-ho," cried the sheep, and Shem, and a
    pair of protozoa:
"We're a-going to roam till we find a home that will
    suit old Father Noah."

There used to be rumors of a country that men
called Atlantis. It was said to lie far out at sea. A

magnificent country. The people there were happier and freer than anywhere else. It was also a land where it was no trouble at all to be rich, and where strangers were treated as equals and welcomed as friends. Until it disappeared so mysteriously it was like an America, a land to which the people of those ancient times longed to go.

I dreamed once that it had not disappeared, after all, but that it was still to be found if you took a long voyage, and that it was happier and freer and finer than ever. And I wanted to go there. I dreamed that America had got itself in such trouble that thousands of people were leaving to live in Atlantis. This part of my dream was a nightmare, and not at all clear, but my recollection is that we'd elected a gangster as President. And he said his understanding was that he'd been elected for life; and when anyone objected to this, he sent the police around either to beat him up or to cut off his head. And after this President had beaten up everyone thoroughly, a great many native Americans who had once despised immigrants decided to sail away and go to work in a new land themselves.

But it wasn't at all easy to emigrate and give up America. In spite of the way that the President beheaded us, we were fond of our country. And we knew if we went to another we mightn't come back. You can imagine how it would feel, perhaps, if you yourself were leaving America, and looking for the last time at all the little things in your room, and walking for the last time in the streets

a porter was sent around to cut off his head

or the fields you knew best. And the day before sailing you would go around seeing your friends, and saying good-bye to them, knowing you wouldn't see them again. And then on the last day you'd sit for a while with your mother, and she would talk of your plans and your comforts, and you'd both be quite calm. And the hour to go would come; and you'd kiss her. And she'd suddenly cling to you. . . .

Then the ship, and the steam-whistles calling, and the gray, endless sea. And you up on deck, day by day, staring out at the waters; and seeing not them but your loved ones, or bits of your home: wondering if you'd been courageous to leave it, or cold, and a fool.

But the sunsets and dawns, and the winds—strong and clean—would bring peace. You would think of the new world you were sailing to, and of how good it would be there, and of how you would prosper, and the long, happy life you would lead. . . . And the voyage would come to an end, and you'd sail up the harbor.

Then at the dock, men in strange clothing would shout orders at you: "Peely wush, okka Hoogs! Peely wush! Okkabab!" and you would dis-

cover that "peely wush" meant hurry up, and that "okka" was a swear word and that when they said "Hoog" they meant you. It would be a comic nickname, you know: as we say Chinks for Chinamen. And they'd hustle you Hoogs off the ship, and shove you around on the pier, and examine your eyes and your pocketbooks, and at last set you free.

And there you would be, in Atlantis, where people were happy.

But you'd find at the start that Atlantis was busy and rough; and parts of the city would be dirty and have a bad smell. And then you would find that the Hoogs mostly lived in those parts, and had to work at pretty nearly anything to pay for their lodging. You'd see Americans that you knew; an ex-senator, perhaps, sewing shirts; and a prominent bishop would be standing in the street peddling shoe-strings. The reason for this would be that until they knew what "okkabab" meant, and could read and write the language of Atlantis, and spell its odd spellings, and pronounce it without too much of an American accent, they couldn't get any but unskilled and underpaid jobs. Meantime they would look to a native like cheap, outlandish peddlers. Even their own fellow-immigrants would try to exploit them. And instead of their finding it easy to get rich, as they'd hoped, they would be so hard up that they'd have to fight like wolves for each nickel.

Your American clothes would be another difficulty, because they'd be laughed at. You'd have to buy and learn to wear the kind of things they wore in Atlantis. And your most polite ways would seem rude in Atlantis, or silly; so you'd have to learn *their* rules of politeness, which would strike *you* as silly. And you'd have to learn habits of living which would often amaze you; and if you were slow to adopt them, they'd class you as stupid. Their ideas of joking would also be different from yours; and you'd slowly and awkwardly discover what was fun in Atlantis.

You'd have to change yourself in so many ways, your old friends wouldn't know you. Pretty soon you wouldn't be an American at all any longer. And yet you would never feel wholly an Atlantisan either. Your children would look down on you as a greenhorn, and laugh at your slips. They would seem unsympathetic, or different,—not quite your own children.

The natives of Atlantis would help you along, once in a while, by giving you lectures and telling you not to read your home paper. But you, who had felt so adventurous and bold, when you started, would have to get used to their regarding you as a comic inferior. Not even your children would know what you had had to contend with. Not one of the natives would try to put himself in your place.

Yet how could they? How could anyone who hadn't gone through the experience? It is a complicated matter to learn to belong to a strange country, when the process includes making yourself over to fit other men's notions.

It was easy for Noah: there was nobody to get used to on Ararat.

AS THEY GO RIDING BY

What kind of men do we think the mediæval knights really were? I have always seen them in a romantic light, finer than human. Tennyson gave me that apple, and I confess I did eat, and I have lived on the wrong diet ever since. Malory was almost as misleading. My net impression was that there were a few wicked, villainous knights, who committed crimes such as not trusting other knights or saying mean things, but that even they were subject to shame when found out and rebuked, and that all the rest were a fine, earnest Y. M. C. A. crowd, with the noblest ideals.

But only the poets hold this view of knights, not the scholars. Here, for example, is a cold-hearted scholar, Monsieur Albert Guérard. He has been digging into the old mediæval records with an unromantic eye, hang him; and he has emerged with his hands full of facts which prove the knights were quite different. They did have some good qualities. When invaders came around, the knights fought them off as nobly at possible; and they often went away and fought Saracens or ogres or such, and when thus engaged they gave little trouble to the good folk at home. But in between wars, not being educated, they couldn't sit still and be quiet. It was dull in the house. They liked action. So they rode around the streets in a pugnacious, wild-western manner, despising anyone who could read and often knocking him down; and making free with the personal property of mer-

chants and peasants, who they thought had no special right to property or even to life. Knights who felt rough behaved as such, and the injuries they inflicted were often fatal.

They must have been terrors. Think of being a merchant or cleric without any armor, and meet-

ing a gang of ironclads, with the nearest police
court centuries off! Why, they might do anything;
and whatever they did to a merchant, they thought
was a joke. Whenever they weren't beating you up
they fought with one another like demons—I don't
mean just in tournaments, which were for practice, but in small, private wars. And to every war,
public or private, citizens had to contribute; and
instead of being thanked for it, they were treated
with the utmost contempt.

Suppose a handsome young citizen, seeing this
and feeling ambitious, tried to join the gang and
become a knight himself. Would they let him? No!
At first, if he were a powerful fighter, he did have
a small chance, but as time went on and the knights
got to feeling more noble than ever, being not
only knights but the sons of knights, they wouldn't
let in a new man. The mere idea made them so
indignant they wanted to lynch him. "Their loath-
ing for the people seemed almost akin in its in-
tensity to color prejudice."

They were also extravagant and improvident
and never made money, so the more they spent, the
more they had to demand from the people. When
everyone had been squeezed dry for miles around,
and had been thumped to make sure, the knights
cursed horribly and borrowed from the Church,
whether the Church would or no, or got hold of

some money-lender and pulled his beard and never paid interest.

The Church tried to make them religious and partly succeeded; there were some Christian knights who were soldierly and courtly, of course. But, allowing for this (and for my exaggerating their bad side, for the moment), they certainly were not the kind of men Tennyson led me to think.

I do not blame Tennyson. He had a perfect right to romanticize. He may have known what toughs the knights were as well as anybody, but loved their noble side, too, and dreamed about it until he had made it for the moment seem real to him, and then hurried up and written his idyls before the dream cracked. He may never have intended me or any of us to swallow it whole. "It's not a dashed bible; it's a book of verse," I can imagine him saying, "so don't be an idiot; don't forget to read your encyclopedia, too."

But verse is mightier than any encyclopedia. At least it prevails. That's because the human race is emotional and goes by its feelings. Why haven't encyclopedists considered this? They are the men I should blame. What is the use of embodying the truth about everything in a precise condensed style which, even if we read it, we can't remember, since it does not stir our feelings? The encyclopedists should write their books over again, in passionate verse. What we need in an encyclopedia is lyrical fervor, not mere completeness—Idyls of Economic Jurisprudence, Songs of the Nitrates. Our present compendiums are meant for scholars rather than people.

Well, the knights are gone and only their armor

and weapons remain; and our rich merchants, who no longer are under-dogs, collect these as curios.

They present them with a magnificent gesture to local museums. The metal suit which old Sir Percy Mortimer wore, when riding down merchants, is now in the Briggsville Academy, which never heard of Sir Percy, and his armor is a memorial to Samuel Briggs of the Briggs Tailoring Company. In Europe a few ancient families, in financial decay, are guarding their ancestors' clothing as well as they can, but sooner or later they will be driven to sell it, to live. And they won't live much longer at that. The race will soon be extinct.

Last year I got a bulletin of the Metropolitan Museum of Art about armor. It described how an American collector saw a fine set in Paris. "A single view was quite enough to enable him to decide that the armor was too important to remain in private hands." And that settled it. These collectors are determined fellows and must have their own way—like the knights.

But there were difficulties this time. They couldn't at first get this set. The knightly owner of the armor, "in whose family it was an heirloom, was, from our point of view, singularly unreasonable: he . . . was unwilling to part with it; the psychological crisis when he would allow it to pass out of his hands must, therefore, be awaited." For there comes "a propitious moment in cases of this kind," adds the bulletin.

Yes, "in cases of this kind" collectors comfortably wait for that crisis when the silent old knightly owner finally has to give in. They leave agents to watch him while he struggles between want and pride, agents who will snap him up if a day comes when the old man is weak. These agents must be persistent and shrewd, and must present tactful arguments, and must shoo away other agents, if possible, so as to keep down the price. When the "propitious" time comes they must act quickly, lest the knight's weakness pass, or lest some other knight send him help and thus make them wait longer. And, having got the armor, they hurry it off, give a dinner, and other merchants come to view it and measure it and count up the pieces.

This sort of thing has been happening over and over in Europe—the closing scenes of the order of knighthood, not foreseen at gay tournaments! They were lucky in those days not to be able to look into the future. Are *we* lucky to be blind, at Mount Vernon or on some old campus? The new times to come may be better—that always is possible—but they won't be the kind we are building, and they may scrap our shrines.

Some day when our modern types of capitalists are extinct, in their turn, will future poets sing of their fine deeds and make young readers dream? Our capitalists are not popular in these days, but the knights weren't in theirs, and whenever abuse grows extreme a reaction will follow. Our critics and reformers think *they* will be the heroes of song, but do we sing of critics who lived in the ages of chivalry? There must have been reformers then who pleaded the cause of down-trodden citizens, and denounced and exposed cruel knights, but we don't know their names. It is the knights we re-remember and idealize, even old Front-de-Bœuf. They were doers—and the men of the future will idealize ours. Our predatory interests will seem to them gallant and strong. When a new Tennyson appears, he will never look up the things in our newspapers; he won't even read the encyclopedia—Tennysons don't. He will get his conception of capitalists out of his heart. Mighty men who built towers to work in, and fought with one another, and engaged in great capitalist wars, and stood high above labor. King Carnegie and his round directors' table of barons of steel. Armour, Hill and Stillman, Jay Gould—musical names, fit for poems.

The men of the future will read, and disparage their era, and wish they had lived in the wild clashing times we have now. They will try to enliven the commonplaceness of their tame daily lives by getting up memorial pageants where they can dress up as capitalists—some with high hats and umbrellas (borrowed from the museums), some as golfers or polo players, carrying the queer ancient implements. Beautiful girls will happily unbuckle their communist suits and dress up in old silken low-necks, hired from a costumer. Little boys will look on with awe as the procession goes by, and then hurry off to the back yard and play they are great financiers. And Readers will sigh if some book says that capitalists were not all noble, but a mixed human lot, like the knights.

IT'S ONLY OLD CHARLIE

The two most picturesque sights in Mezca, when I stopped at the Cape, were two natives who walked around talking to themselves all the time. They talked about the state of the tribe, and sometimes of the world. As each had his own ideas about this, they usually went around separately. One of them wore a large bulging mask, resembling the head of a Drum Fish, and he liked to have his views referred to as the Great Drum Fish's views. As to the other native, he delivered *his* addresses perched on tall stilts, and spoke with a dignified bellow, and called himself Truth.

These two rivals, between them, had in a way hypnotized the inhabitants. People not only listened to their opinions, and let them scold them, but paid them for doing it. They didn't pay them well (these two men were most sarcastic about this) and they didn't often listen attentively to what the men said. But it seemed to impress them to have a Great Drum Fish around.

In fact he was so much a public character that I supposed, when he died, they would hold some kind of general election to choose his successor. But not at all; a young native came along named

Charlie Zam, who bought the mask from the family and became the Great Drum Fish by purchase.

In the old Hebrew days when a man wished to behave in this way, yet, not being a priest or a ruler, had no public standing, he went off to some place in the desert and dressed up in goat-skins, and then he presently came back to town and said

that he was a prophet. Any political opinions he
was full of, he said, were the Lord's.

This interested everyone, even the rulers and
priests. If he had just walked around and talked
naturally to the crowd, man to man, he wouldn't

Give ear,
O Earth!

have been impressive—unless his views made him
so, gradually. And that gradual way is too slow for
a man in a hurry, as men with opinions that they
wish to express mostly are. But when he declared
these were the Lord's views, that got him a hearing. So he spoke in an oracular manner and put

dust on his head, and danced and rent his garments in twain, and got everyone scared, and then expressed whatever dislike he happened to feel toward the government. He would get up and shout at the top of his voice, "Give ear, O Earth! This people are an offense and an abomination! Thus saith the Lord."

If he hadn't put in "Thus saith the Lord" quickly, the crowd might have stoned him; in fact they did anyhow sometimes, not liking abuse. But they certainly stood a lot of it, first and last, for there were no end of prophets, and they mostly were irascible men who wanted the world changed at once.

One prophet, Jeremiah, a most positive old man with a short temper, used to become especially exasperated, when his advice wasn't taken. "I will send serpents, cockatrices, among you, and they shall bite you," he'd howl, with great fierceness; and hurriedly add, "saith the Lord." (Jer. viii, 17.)

Nowadays, when some private citizen feels public-spirited, and wants to say "Woe, Woe," to other citizens, and "Beware," and all that, he too feels an instinct to be as impressive as can be about it. One obvious way to be impressive is to become a great man. Another is merely to seem one. The modern Jeremiah or Charlie Zam accordingly sets up a newspaper, and talks his opinions into a printing press as fast as he can; and then instead of signing them Jeremiah, he signs them The Editor.

The Editor is a self-bestowed title, yet people respect it. They observe that any man who is an editor takes himself very seriously. And not only himself but other editors—he takes them all seri-

ously—they all pretend to take each other that way, the same as kings used to do. They quarrel, and they criticize each other, but that doesn't hurt—the main thing is for each of them to speak of himself by his title, and never allude to himself as "I" or to his views as "my" views, but to call himself "We," so as to make himself sound like a king.

On top of this, he gives himself still another title, or name. He decides that he will call himself The Times, or The Herald or Statesman. He then goes out and tells the postman that if mail comes addressed to The Statesman, the postmaster is to be sure to deliver it to him, Charlie Zam. And thereafter he alludes to himself as The Statesman, in whatever he prints. If he comes down to the office feeling peevish about the day's news, he sits at

He decides to call himself The Statesman

his typewriter and writes, "It is The Statesman's opinion that the government is playing with fire. We entertain grave objections," says Charlie, "to the Cabinet's views. Frankly," he says, "we are obliged to dissent from them wholly." And after having carried on in this magnificent manner all day, he brushes the dust off his hat, and he gets on the street car, and pays the conductor his nickel, and goes home to his wife.

I don't know just what goes on in the head of a man who does this. I'm told that sometimes he calls himself The Statesman or The Times out of modesty. He feels that it would be too much to ask everybody to listen to him, Charlie Zam; but it's all right to do so, of course, if he says he's The Times.

If you get him to arguing he will give you all the reasons you like. As near as I can understand, he has too much respect for the Dignity of the Press and of Journalism, to—er—well, to admit that his editorials are by himself. The idea is that a Drum Fish is a more dignified thing than a man. "Our wish," he will tell you, still hanging on to the first person plural, "is to make our paper an organ of ideas, and not one of personalities. We feel that to print signed editorials would defeat our whole purpose." (The old ostrich theory. If a man sits in an office and says he's The Times, that makes his opinions impersonal.)

An organ of ideas, run by men, is not a realistic conception. A harsh judge would call it dishonest; a kind one pathetic. These "organs" that pretend to be other than human are frauds. Their combats on economics and politics are the voices of men, with irregular tempers, and pet hopes or schemes, and far from impersonal insight, and jerky digestions.

When these voices are supposed to come from things called The Star or The Globe, the effect on the rest of us nevertheless is hypnotic. It's only old Charlie parading around, and deploring and roaring, and pretending he isn't just Charlie, and we ought to smile and pass on. But, somehow, when he behaves that way he sounds important. It works.

So he speaks of himself as The Statesman, and uses the "We," and struts most imposingly around in the world of today. Perhaps in the world of tomorrow there'll be less masquerading. Imagine the amusement with which they'll look back on our landscape and study these picturesque figures marching grandly about it—The Argus, The Guardian, The Sentinel, The Tribune, The Sun.

THE HEART OF MAN

The heart of man is capable of
Forty ridiculous kinds of love,
And the heart of woman is just an ocean
Of jealous, immoderate, damp devotion.

BUFFOON FATE

Suppose that a lot of us were living aboard a huge ship. Suppose the ship didn't rock much, or require any urgent attention, but kept along on an even keel and left us free to do as we liked. And suppose we got into the habit of staying below more and more, never coming up on deck or regarding the sea or the sky. Just played around below, working at little jobs; eating, starving, quarreling, and arguing in the hold of that ship.

And then, maybe, something would happen to call us on deck. Some peril, some storm. And we'd suddenly realize that our life between decks wasn't all. We'd run up and rub our eyes, and stare around at the black waters, the vast, heaving waves; and a gale from far spaces would strike us, and chill us like ice. And we'd think, "By God, we're on a ship! And where is our ship sailing?"

Wars, plagues and famines are the storms that make us run up on deck. They snatch us up, out of our buying and selling and studying, and show us our whole human enterprise as a ship, in great danger.

We want to scurry back below, where it's lighted and smaller. Down below where our toys are. On deck it's too vast, too tremendous. . . .

We want to forget that the human race is on an adventure, sailing no one knows where, on a magical, treacherous sea.

We have fought our way up from being wild, houseless lemurs, or lower, and little by little we have built up our curious structure—of learning, of art, of discovery—a wonderful structure: at least for us monkey-men. It has been a long struggle. We can guess, looking backward, what our ancestors had to contend with—how the cavemen fought mammoths, and their tough sons and daughters fought barbarism. But we want to forget it. We wish everyone now to be genial. We pretend that this isn't the same earth that our ancestors lived on, but quite a different planet, where roughness is kept within bounds and where persons wear gloves and have neat wooden doors they can lock.

But it's the very same earth that old Grandpa Caveman once wrestled with, and where old Grandma Cavewoman ran for her life twice a week.

We've varnished the surface.

But it's still wild and strange just beneath.

In a prophetic book called *The War in the Air,* by H. G. Wells, he pictured the world swimming along quietly, when bang! a war starts! And it spreads, and takes in East and West, smashes cities, stops everything. And one of the young men in the story looks around rather dazed, and says in a low voice: "I've always thought life was a lark, It isn't. This sort of thing has always been happening, I suppose—these things, wars and earthquakes, that sweep across all the decency of life. It's just as though I had woke up to it all for the first time. . . . And it's always been so—it's the way of life."

So that's what we need to get used to, that it's *that* kind of a ship. We ought to have a sense of the adventure on which we're all bound.

It's not only war—not by a long shot—that gives men that sense. Great scientists have it. Great sailors. You can sort out the statesmen around you, the writers, the poets, according to whether or not they ever have been up on deck.

Theodore Dreiser has, for instance; Arnold Bennett had not. Charles Dickens had not, and that's why he is ranked below Thackeray. Compare James Joyce's *Portrait of the Artist* with George Moore's *Confessions,* and if you apply this criterion, Moore takes a back seat.

There's one great man now gone, however, who had almost too much of this sense: this cosmic adventure emotion. And that man was Joseph Conrad. Perhaps in his youth the sea came upon him too suddenly, or his boyhood sea-dreams awed too deeply his then unformed mind. At all events, the men in his stories are like lonely spirits, sailing, spellbound, through the immense forces surrounding the world. "There they are," one of them says, as he stands at the rail, "stars, sun, sea, light, darkness, space, great waters; the formidable Work of the Seven Days, into which man seems to have blundered unbidden. Or else decoyed."

We all have that mood. But Conrad was given to brooding. And his habit at night when he stood staring up at the stars was to see (or conjure up rather) a dumb buffoon Fate, primeval, unfriendly and stupid, whom Man must defy. And Conrad defied it, but wearily, for he felt sick at heart,— because of his surety that Fate was ignoble, and blind.

It's as though he had told himself ghost stories about this great universe. He felt that it ought to have a gracious and powerful master, leading men along fiery highways to test but not crush them, and marching them firm-eyed and glorious toward high goals. But instead there was nothing. The gray, empty wastes of the skies beyond starland were silent. Or, worse, their one sound was the footfall of that buffoon Fate.

The way to meet this black situation, according to Conrad, is to face it with grim steady courage. And that's what he did. It's stirring to discover the fineness of this man's tragic bravery. But when I get loose from his spell, and reflect, independently, I ask myself, "After all, was this performance so brave?"

We must all weigh the universe, each in his own penny-scales, and decide for ourselves whether to regard it as inspiring or hollow. But letting our penny-scales frighten us isn't stout-hearted.

If I were to tell myself ghost stories until I was trembling, and then, with my heart turning cold, firmly walk through the dark, my courage would be great but not admirable. And it was that way with Conrad. His courage was splendid—but after all for what did he use it? To bear with magnificent fortitude his self-conjured dreads.

THE ENJOYMENT OF
GLOOM

☼

There used to be a poem—I wish I could find it again—about a man in a wild, lonely place who had a child and a dog. One day he had to go somewhere. So he left the dog home to protect the child until he came back. The dog was a strong, faithful animal, with large, loving eyes.

"Keep all the wolves out now."

—186—

The Enjoyment of Gloom

Something terrible happened soon after the man had gone off. I find I'm rather hazy about it, but I think it was wolves. The faithful dog had an awful time of it. He fought and he fought. He was pitifully cut up and bitten. In the end, though, he won.

The man came back when it was night. The dog was lying on the bed with the child he had saved. There was blood on the bed. The man's heart stood still. "This blood is my child's," he thought hastily, "and this dog, which I trusted, has killed it." The dog feebly wagged his tail. The man sprang upon him and slew him.

He saw his mistake immediately afterward, but —it was too late.

When I first read this I was a boy of perhaps ten or twelve. It darn near made me cry. There was one line especially—the poor dog's dying howl of reproach. I think it did make me cry.

I at once took the book—a large, blue one—and hunted up my younger brothers. I made them sit one on each side of the nursery fire. "I'm going to read you something," I said.

They looked up at me trustfully. I remember their soft, chubby faces.

I began the poem, very much moved; and they, too, soon grew agitated. They had a complete confidence, however, that it would come out all right. When it didn't, when the dog's dying howl came, they burst into tears. We all sobbed together.

Reading about the poor dog.

This session was such a success that I read it to them several times afterward. I didn't get quite so much poignancy out of these encores myself but my little brothers cried every time, and that, somehow, gave me pleasure. It gave no pleasure to them. They earnestly begged me not to keep reading it. I was the eldest, however, and paid little attention, of course, to their wishes. They'd be playing some game, perhaps. I would stalk into the room, book in hand, and sit them down by the fire. "You're going to read us about the dog again?" they would wail. "Well, not right away," I'd say. "I'll read something funny to start with." This didn't much cheer them. "Oh, please don't read us about the dog, please don't," they'd beg, "we're playing run-around." When I opened the book they'd begin crying 'way in advance, long before that stanza came describing his last dying howl.

It was kind of mean of me.

There was a famous old author, though, who did nothing but that all his life. I mean Thomas Hardy. Dying howls, of all kinds, were his specialty.

His critics have assumed that from this they

can infer his philosophy. They say he believed that "sorrow is the rule and joy the exception," and that "good-will and courage and honesty are brittle weapons" for us to use in our defense as we pass through such a world.

I'm not sure that I agree that that was his philosophy. It's fair enough to say that Hardy's stories, and still more his poems, paint chiefly the gloomy and hopeless situations in life, just as Mark Twain and Aristophanes painted the comic ones. But Mark Twain was very far from thinking the world was a joke, and I doubt whether Hardy regarded it at heart as so black.

He wrote—about how many books? twenty odd? —novels and poems. They make quite an edifice. They represent long years of work. Could he have been so industrious if he had found the world a chamber of horrors? He might have done one or two novels or poems about it, but how could he have kept on if he had truly felt the whole thing was hopeless? He kept on, because although sorrows moved him he did not feel their weight. He found he could have a good time painting the world's tragic aspects. He is somehow or other so constituted that that was his pleasure. And he wanted his own kind of pleasure, just as you and I want our kinds. That's fair.

I like to think that the good old soul had a lot of fun all his life, describing all the gloomiest episodes a person could think of. If a good, gloomy episode came into his mind while he was shaving, it brightened the whole day, and he bustled off to set it down, whistling.

Somebody once asked him if he were as pessimistic as his writings would indicate, and he replied that it wasn't safe to judge a man's thoughts by his writings. His writings showed only what kind of things he liked to describe. "Some authors become vocal before one aspect of life, some another." (Perhaps not his exact words but close to it.) One aspect of life may impress you, yet leave you in silence; another may stimulate you into saying something; but what does that prove? It merely shows what you like best to talk about, not your philosophy. A cat whose life is principally peace and good food and warm fires makes hardly any noise about those things—at most a mere purr. But she does become vocal, and wildly so, over midnight encounters. If another cat so much as disputes her way on a fence-top, her tragic shrieks of anguish will sound like the end of the world. Well, Mr. Hardy spent his life in what was chiefly a peaceful era of history, in a liberal and prosperous country; and he personally, too, had his blessings—the blessing of being able, for instance, to write really good books, and the blessing of finding a public to read and admire them. Was any of this reflected in his themes, though? Did he purr? Mighty little. No, he preferred looking around for trouble in this old world's back yards; he prowled about at night till he came upon some good hunk of bleakness, and then he sat down, like the cat, to utter long-drawn-out wails, which gave him strange, poignant sensations of deep satisfaction. They gave us quite other sensations but he didn't care. In the morning he cantered back in, pleased and happy, for breakfast, and he basked in the sun, blinking sagely, the rest of the day. And we say, with respect, "A great pessimist; he thought life was all sorrow."

The principal objection to pessimists is they sap a man's hope. As some English writer has said, there are two kinds of hope. First, the hope of success, which gives men daring, and helps them win against odds. That isn't the best sort of hope. Many deliberately cultivate it because it makes for success, but that is an insincere habit; it's really self-hypnotism. It may help us to win in some particular enterprise, yes; but it's dangerous, like drug-taking. You must keep on increasing the dose, and blindfolding your reason. Men who do it are buoyant, self-confident, but some of their integrity is lost.

The best kind of hope is not about success in this or that undertaking. It's far deeper; hence when things go against you, it isn't destroyed. It is hope about the nature and future of man and the universe. It is this hope the pessimists disallow. That's why they repel us. Some lessen our hope in the universe; others, in man.

THE WRONG LAMPMAN

It is odd, or no, it's not, but it's note-worthy, that Shaw has had few disciples. Here is a witty, vivacious man, successful and keen: why isn't he the head of a school of other keen, witty writers? He has provided an attractive form—the play with an essay as preface. He has provided stock characters, such as the handsome-hero male-moth, who protests so indignantly at the fatal attraction of candles. He has developed above all that useful formula which has served many a dramatist—the comic confrontation of reason and instinct in man. Yet this whole apparatus lies idle, except for the use that Shaw makes of it. It is as though after Ford had perfected an automobile, no one had taken a drive in it, ever, but Ford.

The explanation that Shaw's is too good a machine, or that it takes a genius to run it, is not sufficiently plausible. The truth probably is that his shiny car has some bad defect.

It has this defect certainly: in all his long arguments, Shaw has one underlying assumption—that men could be perfectly reasonable and wise if they would. They have only to let themselves; and if they won't it's downright perversity. This belief is at the center of his being, and he can't get away from it. He doesn't hold it lightly: he's really in earnest about it. Naturally, when he looks around at the world with that belief in his heart, and sees men and women making blunders which he thinks they don't need to, he becomes too exasperated for silence, and pours out his plays. Sometimes he is philosophic enough to treat his fellows amusedly; sometimes he is serious and exacerbated, in which case he is tiresome. But at heart he is always provoked and astonished at men for the way they fend off the millennium, when it's right at their side.

He may have inherited this attitude from those economists who flourished, or attempted to flourish, in the generation before him—those who built with such confidence on rationalism in human affairs. Man was a reasonable being, they said and believed; and all would be well with him, therefore, when he once saw the light. To discover the light might be difficult, but they would do all that for us, and then it would surely be no trouble to man to accept it. They proceeded to discover the light in finance, trade, and matters of government; and Shaw, coming after them, extended the field into marriage, and explained to us the rational thing to do in social relations. These numerous doses of what was confidently recommended as reason were faithfully swallowed by all of us; and yet we're not changed. The dose was as pure as these doctors were able to make it. But—reason needs admixtures of other things to be a good dose. Men feel that without these confirmings it's not to be trusted.

The turn that psychology has taken during the last twenty years has naturally been unlucky for Shaw as a leader, or influence. He appears now as the culminating figure of an old school of thinkers, instead of the founder of a new. And that old school is dead. It was so fascinated by reason, or what it believed to be such (for we should not assume that its conceptions, even of reason, were right), that it never properly studied or faced human nature.

Civilization is a process, not a trick to be learned overnight. It is a way of behavior which we super-animals adopt bit by bit. The surprising and hopeful thing is that we adopt it at all. Civilization is the slow modification of our old feral qualities, the slow growth of others, which we test, then discard or retain. An occasional invention seems to hasten things, but chiefly externally; for the internal change in men's natures is slower than glaciers, and it is upon the sum of men's natures that civilization depends. While this testing and churning and gradual molding goes on, some fellow is always holding up a hasty lamp he calls reason, and beckoning the glacier one side, like a will-o'-the-wisp.

Shaw's lamp of reason is one that has an extra fine glitter; it makes everything look perfectly simple; it shows us short-cuts. He recommends it as a substitute for understanding, which he does not manufacture. Understanding is slow, and is always pointing to the longest way round.

Shaw has studied the ways of mankind, but without enough sympathy. It is unlucky, both for him and for us, this is so. If he had been humorous and wise, what a friend he'd have been to us. Instead, being brilliant and witty, he has remained an outsider, a man with a warm-blooded brain and a gray-matter heart.

THE SEAMY SIDE OF FABRE

This is an essay on Fabre—that lovable and charming old Frenchman who wrote about insects. *I* don't say he's lovable, mind you, but that's how he is always described.

He was one of those fortunate men who are born with a gift of some sort. His gift was for interpretation, but it worked well in only one field. Every animal, vegetable and mineral finds an interpreter, sooner or later; some man who so loves them that he understands them and their story, and finds ways of telling it to the rest of mankind—if they'll let him. Fabre was born with a peculiar understanding of insects.

Even as a baby he was fascinated by grasshoppers and beetles. As a child he wished to study them far more than anything else. He should have been encouraged to do this; allowed to, at any rate. Any child with a gift, even for beetles, should be allowed to develop it. But this small boy was born in a place where his gift was despised; he was torn away from his insects and put through the mill.

Our great blundering old world is always searching for learning and riches, and everlastingly crushing underfoot all new riches and learning. It tried to make Fabre, a born lover of nature, desert her; it forced him to teach mathematics for decades instead. The first thing the world does to a genius is to make him lose all his youth.

Well, Fabre, after losing his youth, and his middle age too, and after being duly kept back at every turn, all his life, by the want of a few extra francs, finally won out at sixty. That is to say, he then got a chance to study and write about insects, in a tiny country home, with an income that was tinier still. "It is a little late, O my pretty insects," he said; "I greatly fear the peach is offered to me only when I'm beginning to have no teeth wherewith to eat it."

As it turned out, however, this wasn't true. He had not only plenty of time, but in my opinion, too much. He lived to be over ninety and he wrote and he wrote and he wrote: he wrote more about insects than any one man or woman can read. I consider it lucky that he didn't begin until sixty.

Insects, as everyone knows, are the worst foes of man. Fabre not only studied these implacable beings but loved them. There was something unnatural about it; something disloyal to the whole human race. It is probable that Fabre was not really human at all. He may have been found in some human cradle, but he was a changeling. You can see he has insect blood in him, if you look at his photograph. He is leathery, agile, dried up. And his grandmother was waspish. He himself always felt strangely close to wasps, and so did wasps to him. I dare say that in addition to Fabre's *Life of*

Which shall the Future belong to — man or the Insects?

the Wasp, there exists, if we could only get at it, a wasp's Life of Fabre.

If the wasp wrote as Fabre does, he would describe Fabre's birth, death, and matings, but tell us hardly anything else about Fabre's real life. He would dwell chiefly on Fabre's small daily habits and his reactions to the wasp's interference.

"Desirous of ascertaining what the old Fabre would do if stung," writes the wasp, "I repeatedly stuck my sting in his leg—but without any effect. I afterward discovered however I had been stinging his boots. This was one of my difficulties, to tell boots and Fabre apart, each having a tough wizened quality and a powdery taste.

"The old Fabre went into his wooden nest or house after this, and presently sat down to eat one of his so-called meals. I couldn't see an atom of dung on the table however, and though there were some fairly edible flowers he never once sucked them. He had only an immense brown root called a potato, and a 'chop' of some cow. Seizing a prong in his claws, the old Fabre quickly harpooned this 'chop' and proceeded to rend it, working his curious mandibles with sounds of delight, and making a sort of low barking talk to his mate. Their marriage, to me, seemed unnatural. Although I watched closely for a week this mate laid no eggs for him: and instead of saving food for their larvæ they ate it all up themselves. How strange that these humans should differ so much from us wasps!"

Another life of Fabre that we ought to have is one by his family. *They* were not devoted to insects; they probably loathed them; and yet they had to get up ever morning and spend the whole day nursing bugs. I picture them, yawning and snarling over the tedious experiments, and listening desperately to Fabre's coleopterous chatter. The members of every famous man's family ought

to give us their side of it. I want more about Tolstoy by Mrs. Tolstoy. And a Life of Milton by his
daughters. That picture of those unfortunate
daughters, looking so sweet and devoted, taking
the blind poet's dictation, is—must be—deceptive.
They were probably wanting to go off upstairs, all
the time, and try new ways of doing their hair; or
go out and talk their heads off with other girls, or
look in shop windows: anything but take down old
Mr. Milton's poetry all day. They didn't know
their papa was a classic: they just thought that he
was the longest-winded papa in their street. I have
no warrant for saying this, I may add. Except that
it's human nature. . . .

Fabre has his good points. He is imaginative and
dramatic, and yet has a passion for truth. He is a
philosopher, an artist. And above all he is not sentimental. He is fond of his insects, but he never is
foolishly fond. And sometimes the good old soul
is as callous as can be toward caterpillars. He shows
no more bowels toward caterpillars than do his
own wasps. Take, for instance, that experiment
when he kept some on the march for eight days,
watching them interestedly as they died of exhaustion. Or his delight at the way caterpillars are
eaten by the Eumenes wasp.

This wasp shuts its egg up in a large, prison-like
cell, with a pile of live caterpillars beside it, to

serve as its food, first half-paralyzing these victims
so they will keep still. Alive but unable to move,
the caterpillars lie there till the grub hatches out.
(Dead caterpillars wouldn't do because this little
grub loves fresh meat.)

The grub, hanging by a thread from the ceiling,
now begins having dinner. "Head downward it is
digging into the limp belly of one of the caterpillars," says Fabre. "The caterpillars grow restless," he adds. (There's a fine brutal touch!) The
grub thereupon, to Fabre's delight, climbs back up
its thread. It is only a baby; it's tender; and when
those wretched caterpillars get to thrashing
around, they might hurt the sweet infant. Not till
"peace" is restored, Fabre adds, does Baby dare to
come down again. Hideous infantile epicure! It
takes another good juicy bite.

And if its dinner moans again, or wriggles, it
again climbs back up.

Imagine some caterpillar reader shuddering at
this horror—this lethal chamber where prominent
caterpillars are slowly eaten alive. Yet scenes like
this occur all through Fabre, and are described
with great relish. If he wrote of them in a dry professional way, it would sound scientific, and I could
read it in a cool, detached spirit with never a
flutter. But he does it so humanly that you get to
be friends with these creatures, and then he springs

some grisly little scene on you that gives you the creeps, and explains to you that the said little scene is going on all the time; and it makes you feel as though there were nothing but red fangs in the world.

Fabre at one time was offered the post of tutor to Napoleon III's son, but he preferred to live in poverty in the country, where he could keep up his studies. No money, no honors could tempt him away from his work. Perhaps this was noble. But it seems to me he made a mistake. In fact, this was the greatest and most fatal mistake of his life.

If he had gone to Napoleon, he might have moped awhile at first, and felt guilty. But he would

They were said to cure lethargy

have gone right on loving insects and wanting to study them. Hence he would have soon begun looking around the palace for specimens. And this might have led to his discovering riches indoors.

Suppose he had written about that bug that takes its name from our beds, and helped us to understand its persistent devotion to man. According to Ealand, the scientist, they are not wholly bad. They were once supposed to be good for hysteria if taken internally. The Ancients gave seven to adults and four to children, he says, "to cure lethargy." But the best Ealand can do is to give us bits of information like this, whereas Fabre, if he had lived in his bedroom, could have been their interpreter.

That's his failure—his books are overweighted with bugs of the fields. I have plowed through long chapters without getting away for a minute from beetles. In bugs of the field I take a due interest (which, I may add, isn't much), but the need of humanity is to know about bugs of the home.

OUR SOFT-HEADED
FRIENDS

There are some people who can't enjoy fairy-stories and don't like imagining. They are a bit too hard-headed. I don't blame such people; they are all right enough in their way. Only they ought not to go around saying fairy-stories are silly. They ought simply to let them alone and live nice hard-headed lives.

It is the same way with soft-headed people who cannot enjoy the real world. Not having much

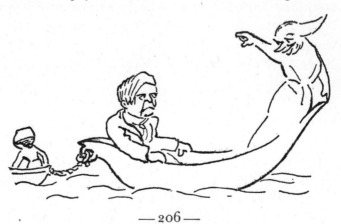

taste for it, and not getting on too well in it, they are apt to call it pretty bad names and to wish it were different. I think them too hasty. Before they abuse or advise it they should first understand it. If they can't, they should let it alone more, and live in their dreams.

Or in those of such dreamers as Maeterlinck, Dunsany, or Poe.

The Maeterlinck books constitute quite a beautiful country. They have long been a favorite home for our soft-headed friends. And those of us who are of a compound between hard and soft enjoy visiting the Maeterlinck coast as we might a resort. It is pleasantly unreal; it is varied. Gentle breezes of sweetness; blue seas, massive rocks; and storms too. Here and there a crag, or dark castle of terrible grandeur. Is it not picturesque? Don't poke at the castles with your umbrella; you might go through the tin; but take it all in the right spirit as you would Coney Island.

Human nature being what it is, there is certainly a need for this place.

There is one little difficulty about the situation however. Monsieur Maeterlinck, the proprietor, although he made his home in this region, liked sometimes to visit the real world, if but for a change. This would have been nothing to object to, though for him injudicious, but he was such a stranger there that he did not at all know his place. He took himself seriously at his home; it was natural, I'm sure; but it led him to speak in the real world with a voice of authority. He was not in the least offensive about it, no one was ever more gentle, but he didn't at all realize that his rank here forbade such a tone. On the Maeterlinck coast, in the realms of romance, he was king. In the real world his judgments were not above those of a child.

It would give me more pleasure (or at any rate it ought to, I know) to dwell on his many abilities than on this one fault. But this excellent man had the misfortune to resemble wood-alcohol. Wood-alcohol is a respectable liquid; it is useful in varnish; when poured in a lamp it heats tea; yes, it has its good side. Yet how little we dwell on its uses, how much on its defect; its one small defect that it's fatal when taken internally.

Maeterlinck all his life made a business of beautiful thoughts. With some of them he built romantic tales that are or were a refreshment. But others he embodied in sermons addressed to reality. He told us none needed to go to his coast for romance, or for purity and beauty and goodness, for we really were full of them. We were made in fact of just these ingredients, at least in our hearts; and it followed, he said, that our actions should be chosen accordingly. Without ever having learned anything much of mankind, he described just the way that he felt all mankind should behave. He put on the robes of a sage, and he sweetened his looks, and his voice became tender and thrilling and rather impressive; and he wrote about the Treasure of the Humble, and Wisdom and Destiny.

The real world is not easy to live in. It is rough; it is slippery. Without the most clear-eyed adjustments we fall and get crushed. A man must stay sober: not always, but most of the time. Those of us who drink from the flasks of the sages of dreamland become so intoxicated with guff we are a peril to everyone.

We trust in peace treaties for instance, on the eve of great wars.

The flask that Wood-Alcohol Maurice, if I may so call him, held so long to our lips in the years before 1914, produced the usual effects of joy first, and then blindness and coma. I speak from experience. I took some myself and was poisoned, and I knew other cases. But it poisoned poor Maeterlinck more—I may say, most of all—for he had taken his own medicine honorably as fast as he mixed it. Owing to this imprudence, he found himself, in 1914, in such a deep coma it almost killed him to come out of it. His anger at having to wake up and face things was loud. He found himself compelled to live for a while in the midst of hard facts, and his comments upon them were scathing; as all dreamers' are.

After a while he made his way back to the land of romance, and if he had stayed there I should have said nothing against him. He was one of the masters of fancy. He could mine fairy gold. But habits are strong, especially bad ones. He couldn't reform. He kept right on sending us his mail-order lessons in sweetness, and musically urging us to live on his moonshine and dreams.

STILL READING AWAY

Still reading away at your paper?
   Still sitting at editors' feet?
      (Clay feet!)
Oh, why do you muse on their views on the news,
   When breezes are sweet in the street?
There's a bit of a cloud flying by in the sky.
   Tomorrow 'twill be far away.
There's a slip of a girl, see her dance to my song!
   Tomorrow she'll be old and gray.
      Come along!
There's music and sunshine and life in the street,
   But ah, you must take them today.

GROWING UP

In 1766 a young Englishman, a clergyman's son, sailed away to seek his fortune in India. There, in spite of his youth, he was given the command of an unruly province. By the time he was twenty-seven he had conquered it, made a fortune by trading, and gone back to England, to live the life of a well-to-do country squire without further toil.

Six of his sons went to India, hoping to repeat his experience. None of them did. Some died in battle, some from the climate, and one died of drink.

One of these active young soldiers, who had himself conquered a province as his father had done, fell in love with and married the most beautiful English girl in Calcutta. A few years later he died, like his brothers. He left a son four years old.

This little boy had some unhappy times after that. His mother carefully dispatched him in charge of a black Indian servant to England, where he was shuttled about from one elderly aunt to another. At the great school that he was then sent away to, he got into trouble, because he was near-

sighted and not very strong and not at all good
at games. Also, one of the boys broke his nose for
him, which spoiled his appearance for life. He
didn't mind that so much, because he and the fellow who did it were friends; but the masters
thrashed him severely, and as he was a weakling he
was kicked around and beaten by all the school
bullies for years.

After a while his mother, who had married an
elderly Major, came to England to live. She had become intensely religious; rather harshly so, it
seemed to her son; but he loved her, and he loved
and admired his step-father too.

At college he followed the hounds, drank and
gambled, like other young men of fashion. He had
grown strong, he was now six feet four, and his
chest was broad in proportion. He traveled on the
Continent, loved a princess, and attended court
balls. He was a polished young buck in tight-fitting
trousers strapped under his boots, a long-tailed
coat, a high collar, a big cravat-tie and a monocle.

Soon after he was twenty-one and had come into
possession of the money which his father had left
him, he lost it. A friend of his, a young clergyman,
who had a sleek, sanctified exterior and a smooth
tongue, wheedled him into making an investment
that completely collapsed. Another fellow he
knew, a man of good family, fleeced him on a large

scale at cards. Years later he pointed out this person to one of his friends. "I have not seen that man," he said, "since he drove me down in his cabriolet to my bankers in the City, where I sold out my patrimony and paid it over to him."

Not wishing to live on his step-father, he looked around to see what a suddenly poor youth could do. He had already had a try at the law, but he hadn't worked hard at it. He now turned to journalism in his need. He didn't work hard at that either. Although almost penniless, he was still a young man of fashion at heart. It occurred to him that, as he had always liked drawing, art might be his best bet.

It wasn't. His amateur sketches were lifelike, they were full of freshness and fun, but they were far too unstudied to meet the demands of those days. In his more ambitious moments, when he tried his hand at subjects like Hogarth's, the vein in which he drew was merely facetious, or prudish and weak. He was a splendid young man in his way, but he was very English, and Art with a capital A brought out an inferior side of him. He sniggered at the nude for example, and he sentimentalized beauty. Nevertheless he eagerly went over to Paris to paint.

While there he met a pretty Anglo-Irish girl with whom he fell in love.

This girl's mother had been watching and waiting to get her daughter a husband. She urged the youth to find some steady job at once, so that he could marry. He was vague about this at first. He gave up art and tried to do illustrations, but he sold very few. A man named Charles Dickens, whom nobody had ever heard of before, was writing the adventures of a character whom he called Mr. Pickwick; and the struggling would-be artist made a number of drawings to go with these Pickwick papers. They all were rejected.

He asked his step-father to help him find some good position, to marry on. The kindly old Major hadn't much money left, owing to the failure of a bank out in India, but he precipitately took what he had and bought a newspaper with it, merely in order to make his step-son its French correspondent.

The girl for whose sake all this was so imprudently done was going to be a wonderful wife for him, the young fellow thought. Perhaps for another husband she might have been; but though he didn't see it, she was narrow-minded and she had had a bad training. She had been taught to be an artful young girl by her artful Mamma, who was as bad-tempered and vulgar a harridan as ever came out of Ireland. But Mamma could simper and be genteel when she tried; and neither her temper nor her match-making wiles were visible to the near-sighted young man. As for the girl, she didn't venture to talk much. He was drawn to her by her singing. She sang simple songs, she made eyes at him, she had lovely white arms, and he married her.

He was only twenty-five, and he didn't find out for some months that he had been cheated again.

It was poverty that opened his eyes. The newspaper on which he was dependent had never been a success, and, under his step-father's soldierly management, after nine months it collapsed. When his wife's mother found that he was going down-hill financially, and that his family was ruined, she reviled him so loudly and coarsely that she made his home-life a hell.

He hunted feverishly for a chance to do bits of ill-paid reviewing. His indolence utterly vanished. He set to work and worked hard, and for longer hours than most men would be able to, trying to sell things to magazine editors who felt lukewarm about him.

His young wife bore him two daughters. When one of these babies died, he wrote his mother, "I think of her only as something charming that for a season we were allowed to enjoy." He added that he could not ask to have her come back to a life of degradation and pain.

At the birth of their third little girl, his wife had an attack of insanity. She never recovered.

The elegant young buck was now down at heel, a hack and a drudge. His mother-in-law screamed tirades at him. His wife became sluggish and dense, like a half-witted child. He worked late into the night trying to support her and his two little girls; and as a matter of honor he felt that he must also pay his step-father's debts.

After long years of struggle Thackeray managed to do this, and more. All England began talking about him, and reading his books. Yet when his first great novel appeared, its tone displeased many critics. It was the work of a man who had mellowed, and who had always had a warm heart, but there was a vein of cynicism in it, and sadness, and its name was *Vanity Fair*.

A WILD POLISH HERO AND THE REVEREND LYMAN ABBOTT

The books a man likes best are those with some-body in them like him. I don't say it isn't a pleasure to read about others, but if he too is there it's still better. And when he is the hero—ah! It's like liv-ing a whole extra life.

ah! when I am the hero!

But there is no drawing back, once you put
yourself into some character—you must do all that
he does, no matter how you hate his mistakes. I
remember once identifying myself with a dissolute
Pole, in a novel, who led me a dance that I haven't
forgotten yet. I ought never to have let myself
fancy that I was that fellow. He was moody, excit-

He deceived
the two women

able, he drank more brandy than I was prepared
to; he talked most bombastically. He made the
most pitiful jokes. But what took my eye in him
was this: he was sincere with himself. He was only
twenty-five years of age, but though young, he was
honest. When he was in love with two women he
never dodged facing it squarely. He deceived the
two women, I grant you, but most heroes deceive
themselves, too. They tell themselves some pretty

story in dilemmas like that. This Pole always saw through *his* stories. He questioned his heart, and listened with reasonable honesty to its responses.

Our capacity for analyzing and criticizing our natures is wonderful. When a man is without self-

I'd hate to be a wild animal

awareness, I feel toward him as I do toward animals.

I admire the animals. I am glad I am not one myself—life in the wilds must be awful—but animals are healthy and sound; and some are good, and intelligent. Men who can't analyze themselves may be good and intelligent also. But they are not advanced beings.

The test of a civilized person is first self-awareness, and then depth after depth of sincerity in self-confrontation. "Unhealthy?" Why, certainly! "Risky?" Yes; like all exploring. But unless you are capable of this kind of thinking, what are you? No matter how able or great, you are still with the animals.

Here and there is a person who achieves this in ways of his own. Not through brain-work alone, or most surely, can insight be won. A few have by nature a true yet instinctive self-knowledge. But that takes a pure soul. The tricks of self-deceiving are too many and ingenious for most of us. . . .

Speaking of pure souls, good old Lyman Abbott had one—he used to edit the *Outlook*—although his was unfortunately the kind that was tastelessly pure. He was as wholesome and good as oatmeal is, but the salt was left out. An excellent person but wingless; not stupid, but dull. Yet—there was something about him—he had an attractive integrity. He put on no airs. He was simple, unpretentious, and he was so straightforward he made me respect him.

Many people respected Lyman Abbott. Yet I was surprised to. Well, I had the Rollo books given to me, as a child; I had to read them on Sundays; and the author of those awful volumes was Lyman Abbott's father. He wrote books for the young. People who write books for the young are a tribe by themselves, and little did I suppose I should ever live to respect one.

Rollo was a Sunday-school boy. Lyman Abbott was a Sunday-school man. He combined in himself the excellencies and the colorlessness of the Sunday-school atmosphere. When it comes time to group us as sheep or as goats, I know this, there won't be any question that he was a regular sheep. No capers for him, except the most innocent capers. No tossing of that excellent head, no kicking up of his heels. There wasn't the faintest suspicion of goatiness in him.

Yet it's strange he was so hopeless: he liked certain forms of adventure. He was a bill-collector once. And when Kansas was being settled so bloodily, in our slavery days, he felt wishful to go there. He once did some detective work too, and he greatly enjoyed it. But his tastes were all heavily flavored with moral intentions.

"My recreations," he said in his book, "I took rather seriously. I neither danced nor played cards, and after I joined the church very rarely went to the theater." He liked music, liked playing the organ. He implied that he played it, however, to add to his income. He was a lawyer when he first felt a call in his heart to the ministry. "Had my wife objected to the change I should have remained in the law." He took some ale or porter at times, "under doctor's counsel," but in general he was a total abstainer. ("From both fermented and distilled liquors," he added.) He never once shaved, never smoked. On the other hand, he said, "I had no inclination to be a monk"; when not at work in the evening, "I was likely to be out, perhaps at a concert or a religious or political meeting, perhaps on a social call." His father kept a boarding-school for girls, and that was where Lyman made most of his social calls, as a youth.

He never overdid anything. "It is a wise hygienic rule to spend less strength than one can accumulate." (That seems like the perfect recipe for not being a genius.) A professional hypnotist once told him he was not a good subject. "I never have been," he wrote: "I have passed through some exciting experiences . . . but I have never been swept off my feet. I have never lost my consciousness of self or my self-mastery. I wonder why it is.

I am not conscious of being either especially strong-willed or especially self-possessed."

He read with assiduity, he said, but without avidity. He seemed to live that way, too.

His sermons, he said in his book, had "merit," but were lacking in magnetism. (You can't sweep other people off their feet if you can't be swept off your own.) He liked preaching, however. It came easily to him.

We are all of us so busy with the small bits of life we can envisage, that we don't often think of how much we may fail to take in. Lyman Abbott spent all his time being a purifying influence. Certain other phases of life, accordingly, simply did not exist for him. If romance had ever tried ap-

proaching the Reverend Lyman Abbott, at night, it would have stood no more chance than a rose would against disinfectants.

Suppose that a Board of Eugenics were in charge of this nation, what would they do with the species this man represented? They would see its good qualities—industry, poise, generosity. It would be wrong to exterminate all Dr. Abbotts; it is plain we need some of him. "But," they would reflect, "this species is apt to wax numerous. We must remember Australia and the rabbits. This type might overrun the whole country. We might even have to put up barbed-wire, or shoot the excess, for us to stay human."

My own recommendation is to cross a few specimens with Poles.

> Lyman Abbott, calm and dry,
> With your conscientious eye,
> Can it possibly be true
> He who made the Poles made you?
>
> In the forest, on the beach,
> You kept pondering what to preach.
> Magic nights of piercing beauty,
> You were lecturing on duty.
>
> In your admirable heart
> Lived a Yearning to Impart;

A Wild Polish Hero

In your veins an earnest flood
Of Listerine instead of blood.

Lyman, Lyman, do you think
Had you gambled, tried to drink,
Loved a Countess, lost your soul,
You'd have ever been a Pole?

THE PERSISTENCE
OF PERNEB

�֍

Just what kind of adventures he had while he was
alive no one knows; but those he has had since his
death have been startling.

He was a dignified-looking man. He had a fine,
slightly arched nose, and firm mouth. He married
a lady of somewhat nobler birth than himself; and
one of his sons was a clergyman. So much for his
family.

As to his possessions, he was fortunate. He had
several country estates in ancient Egypt, and a position at court. On one estate he raised onions, on
another figs; and he kept powerful cattle. He used
to go out in a litter to see them.

This isn't an imaginary story. Perneb wasn't
an historical character but he really existed. He
had his work to do and his worries, like everyone
else. One thing that bothered him, for instance,
was the matter of death. People told him that after
death his spirit would keep right on living; and—
this was the awkward part—would continue to wish

food and shelter. It was up to him to make all the arrangements for this before dying.

Perneb put it off and put it off. He planned it out, but he didn't get round to it. There are a good many other things to do while a man is alive. But everyone round him was arranging as best he could for his future, buying land and building mortuary chambers; and at last Perneb did too.

His home was in Memphis, on the west bank of the Nile, south of Cairo. Along the edge of the desert, near by, a cemetery stretched out for miles. It had streets and broad avenues, and long rows of tombs, and some pyramids. Perneb bought a nice plot of land there, near a pyramid, and began to put up a building.

And then before he had got the place ready for himself, Perneb died.

The evidence shows that they had to complete his tomb in a hurry. This was rather unfortunate. Some of the decorations couldn't be finished, some were left out altogether; and the walls of the south part were hastily put up any which way, in a cheap and inferior manner.

Still, it was a good tomb. A stately stone structure, fifty-odd feet long, forty wide, with inner chambers which were high-ceilinged and handsome and cool. There was one reserved especially for Perneb, which no one could enter, the door

being merely a slit in a thick wall of stone. Perneb
didn't need even this slit himself, since he was
now a spirit, but they knew he'd be hungry, and
they wanted the smell of food to drift in to him
when his dinner was ready.

This walled-up chamber was fairly private, but
not private enough for all purposes. It would do
as a sitting-room for the spirit, but not as a bedroom for sleep. So the builders dug down through
the floor and through the building's foundations,
and down and down into the solid rock under the
ground. At a depth of about fifty feet they stopped,
and hewed out a room deep in the rock, a secret
subterranean chamber, which they furnished completely; and when Perneb died they lowered him
down the shaft and laid him to rest in this room.
Then they walled up the door of this hidden place,
and they filled in the shaft, putting back all the
stone which they had excavated, till it was completely sealed up. This was the regular arrangement and it was probably done by Perneb's orders.
He took all the pains that he could to keep
out visitors and he must have supposed he'd
succeeded.

Instead of leaving his fortune to his family or
charities, Perneb left a good part of it to himself;
that is to say, to his tomb. He arranged to endow it,
to make sure he would get proper care. The sala-

ries of several priests were provided for—it is not known how many, but one of Perneb's fellow-officials provided for eight—besides which there were food and drink, and maintenance and repairs, and incense, and so forth. He assigned the income from his fig farm and his onion farm and some other estates to keep the place going forever. He seemed safely fixed.

Generation and generation passed by and the tomb stood in peace. The priests conducted services in it, the farms sent in food. But gradually, as the cemetery grew, the old parts were neglected, and a time came when Perneb's tomb was no longer properly cared for. Thieves began to rummage round in the cemetery at night, to secure things of value. They broke into Perneb's sitting-room chamber and ran off with its ornaments. And as things grew worse they came back and actually dug down into that shaft; yes, dug out all the stone again, and got down into that deep secret bedroom. They hacked at Perneb's sarcophagus and jerked him out and stripped off his gold. They knocked down and broke his little dishes that stood on a shelf. They didn't completely wreck his home, but they looted it, and mussed it all up.

Perneb must have felt done for and shattered. Those were rough days to live in. There were political fights going on in Memphis. Law and order seemed dead. To the conservatives in the cemetery it must have seemed like the end of the world.

Then Memphis decayed. Men grew listless. The sands drifted in. . . .

In jungles it is the rank vegetation that swallows men's work. On seacoasts, the sea. In dry, barren countries it is the sands that sift in from the desert: that thick inland sea which forever is shifting its borders. The old plundered cemetery disappeared, buried from sight.

Perneb's spirit, which had been so unsettled, had a fresh chance to rest. His food and his attendants were gone, but the robbers were too. He wasn't having as luxurious an after-life as he had arranged for, but at least it was quiet enough for a person to sleep.

As the years went on, the city recovered. New kings ruled in Egypt. Also, new vulgar rich men sprang up who seized all the old farms. When these lords needed stone for their edifices, as the quarries were distant, they dug instead in the sand in the cemetery—there were fine old stones there. Every time that they struck the roof of a tomb in their digging they lifted out its great blocks, and carried them off to use for new buildings. It was so much less work.

The earlier plunderers had been bad enough;

but this seemed the end. Many a respectable old spirit was now left with no home at all. Perneb too was in the greatest peril, but just by chance he escaped. A few blocks were taken from his roof, but then the diggers found other structures; and, in turning aside to strip these, they threw the debris and rubble on Perneb's. This saved him. It was not a dignified road to salvation, to be used as a dump; but Perneb accepted it as one of his many adventures.

A great mound of rubbish was left above him which stood there for ages, protecting him far more effectively than anything else could have done. Nobody suspected that there was anything under that dump-heap. Century after century passed, while the cemetery still yielded stone to the lazy, degenerate generations that lived after Perneb's.

For he had belonged to old times. Far older times than King Tut-ankh-amen's. Perneb was born over a thousand years before that usurper. Even in Perneb's day, civilization was getting shoddy. Tombs for instance weren't built as solidly as men once had built them; instead of using blocks of stone for every wall the masons used facings; but nevertheless they weren't half as shoddy as those who came after.

Meanwhile in other countries, other groups of

men grew up with fresh hearts, and created new
beauties, building solidly and well—for a time.
The marble temples of Greece, the statues, the
Parthenon; the Colosseum of Rome; Roman
aqueducts; strong Roman roads running over the
world. Then these mighty men too had their
climax, leaving lesser descendants, who strut
about unabashed, even today, past their ruins. . . .

Along in the eighteen-hundred-and-forties, as
we count the years, Perneb's spirit was again made
uneasy. *He* didn't know what year it was; he looked
at time in a large way, he was getting the geologic
point of view and learning to count time in eras;
but a new era seemed to be coming in, and Perneb
was bothered. Not by his fellow-countrymen this
time, but by a small group of foreigners, who came
poking around in the graveyard, talking about
"archæology."

In the squalid little villages round about, which
were all that was left now of Memphis, these foreigners had noticed many houses built of blocks
from the cemetery—blocks bearing inscriptions or
relief which made each of them precious. The
head foreigner, Lepsius, wrote a letter home:

> "It is really revolting to see how long lines
> of camels from the neighboring villages
> come here daily, and march off again, loaded
> with building stone. . . . Yesterday a beau-

tiful standing pillar, covered with inscriptions, which was just going to be sketched,
was overturned by the robbers behind our
backs. They do not seem to have succeeded
in breaking it to pieces. The people here are
so degenerate that their strength is quite
insufficient, with all their assiduity, to de-
stroy what their great predecessors have
erected."

Those lazy natives hadn't bothered Perneb,
simply because of the dump. But the foreigners
seemed to be especially attracted by dumps. They
kept pecking at his inquisitively. They made Perneb nervous. Lepsius went to work, digging, and
unearthed the tomb right next to Perneb's, cleared
the sand from its chambers, and studied the scenes
on its walls. When he had got through he went
back home one morning without looking farther.
Another escape!

In the next decade a foreigner named Mariette
appeared with more diggers. They cleared several
more tombs, near the dump-heap. And then they
too stopped.

After this, strangely enough, things grew quiet
once more. Half a century drifted by, peacefully.
There was no more disturbance. The new archæo-
logical danger appeared to have ended—or, at
least, to have passed over Perneb, and gone on else-

where. He was probably fast asleep and sure that his troubles were over, when an American Expedition marched in.

The leader of this expedition took a good look at the dump-heap. He ordered his men to attack it. Perneb listened inside. Thud, thud, came the sound of the picks and the spades, growing nearer. Perneb saw that this would be a close call for him; but he was used to close calls. He still had a chance of escaping, as so often before. But no! Those Americans kept on. They found Perneb's roof. One of the blocks had been broken by the weight of the dump-heap. Through this opening, the American expedition let themselves down and dropped in.

Perneb groaned.

They found the chamber half full of sand, and the walls in bad shape. The weight on top had buckled the south wall, which had been badly built to begin with, and it had partly collapsed. But the stately courtyard was still intact and the rooms with colored figures and scenes, and the portrait of Perneb, standing in full dress at the door.

Those painted scenes told the Americans much about Perneb. One scene was a family-group picture, showing Perneb comfortably seated on cushions, and his family all crouching before him in the most subservient manner. A man's family seldom really crouches to him as much as he'd like, but that's no reason why he shouldn't have them painted that way for his pleasure. Perneb had evidently wished to give this tomb of his an ideal home atmosphere. He had even had himself painted large and his wife very small in this picture. A modern psychologist would probably call that an effort to compensate; it would make him suspect that as a matter of fact Perneb was smaller than any of them. But anyhow, he knew how he wanted things to look in his tomb.

Another scene showed him carefully inspecting the food men were bringing him. His secretary stood by, with a piece of papyrus ready for notes. Two other accountants were near, with reports under their arms. The men of Perneb's day were like us, they were fond of good living—they enjoyed dancing and yachting, for instance, and they delighted in banquets. Perneb hadn't expected to do much yachting apparently, or to dance, after death, but he certainly had intended to continue the pleasure of eating. The pictures on the walls show what a banquet he had planned for himself. There are long strings of figures, all walking toward his inner chamber, carrying baskets and jars, and large joints of meat, and live birds, and bread, and trayfuls of figs, and many fruits and drinks, to keep Perneb busy. Some men would have preferred long strings of postmen, bringing them letters from friends; but Perneb was too self-sufficient to care about that. And he must have had a great appetite. He had other figures painted bringing him calves to eat, and gazelles, and whole oxen. Groups of butchers are sharpening their knives, and carving, and saving the blood; a slave is taking the cover off an incense-burner to make the place fragrant. And in addition to this enormous commissary, all for one man, there are pictures of additional piles of food, for him to turn to when needed. One pile, for instance, has lettering above it, describing its contents: "one thousand portions of wild-fowl, one thousand portions of beef, one thousand loaves of bread, one thousand jars of beer."

As the Americans examined things, Perneb's spirit saw they admired his residence. But their admiration was so great that it led to something that filled him with horror. They asked the Egyptian Government to allow them to buy his home, and walk off with it! They wished to take it to America, a land that Perneb had not before heard of; so new a place it had only been discovered a few hundred years.

The government accepted the money, and Perneb lay stunned by this utterly unexpected move on the part of his tomb: that tomb which he had certainly thought would stay where he put it "forever." Bit by bit, the fine-grained limestone blocks were all taken apart. On the backs of them the Americans found the masons' marks, scrawled in red ochre; and finger-prints left by the workmen were still in the mortar. Under a heap of plaster in an inner wall, where a workman had thrown them, were the scattered shells of the nuts he had had for lunch, all those centuries back.

The blocks were packed into six hundred boxes, and loaded on camels. The procession moved slowly away across the hot, empty desert. Imagine the feelings of Perneb at seeing his tomb carted off! Then suddenly he found that he, too, was being packed in a box. He had been sold by the Egyptians, and was going across the desert himself.

Two steamers were waiting at Suez. Perneb and his home went to sea. He sailed all the way through the Mediterranean, and on past Gibraltar, out into a wide, stormy ocean, beyond any land. They came at length to the fierce modern Memphis which men call New York.

In New York, things were active. Learned experts carefully unpacked and treated the stones, to preserve them, so that the change to a strange climate should not make them decay. They worked on them a year. Then workmen began re-erecting the tomb in the Metropolitan Museum.

The Persistence of Perneb

To get room, they had to break open one of the museum's long walls, and construct a special building large enough to house Perneb's old edifice: an edifice which was erected in the lifetime of Noah.

Biographies are interesting, but how short they are when they end with one's death! A necrography of all that comes afterward—that's the real story. Columbus's biography is most incomplete without his necrography. Napoleon's, too: he died as an exile, defeated and lonely; but after that, he left St. Helena in triumph for Paris, receiving more glory than ever, to rest in a shrine.

Perneb's tomb is now a shrine, in one sense. Visitors come at all hours. They walk in and stare at its massive dignity and the scenes on its walls. Perneb ought to be happy and thankful that he has come through so well. But it isn't all sunshine. He had planned to be exclusive, for one thing, and there's none of that now. Anybody at all can come right in without his permission. And another thing: as the statue of Perneb was destroyed by those early plunderers—the one that used to stand in that inner sitting-room in great state—the museum authorities have put in another man's statue instead. When visitors peer in through the slit, what they see is this stranger, making himself entirely at home there, as though he owned the whole business. He is a broad-faced, flat-nosed looking fellow, no resemblance to Perneb; but there he stands in Perneb's nest, like a low-life cuckoo. And those long strings of figures on the walls now bring him Perneb's dinner—the joints of meat and live birds and beer and the trayfuls of figs.

And where then is Perneb? Well, the poor old boy isn't in his tomb any more—he's outside. There was no other place for him. He is outside his front door in a show case.

There isn't much of him—only part of his head and some bones. Those robbers who broke into his bedroom knocked him about pretty hard. But never mind; at least there is some of him left—he's still there.

A museum attendant keeps Perneb company during the day. He leans over the case and sells pamphlets to a mixed lot of visitors. Perneb never sees a familiar face among them. Not a single old friend.

However, at night the museum is closed, and Perneb has a chance to be quiet. Even then there is the mental annoyance of that man in his sitting-room, but that probably isn't the principal thing on Perneb's mind.

He must have learned by this time that great changes come unforeseen, and that the life of the average museum is only a few hundred years.

New York's may last longer—it might last, say, a couple of thousand. But that's only chicken feed, to Perneb. What will come after that? Will he then be carried away to some other distant civilization? Suppose they took his tomb and that stranger and left him behind?

Well, that's all—so far—of this story. Perneb hears us moderns talking resignedly about dust to dust, like a lot of ephemeral insects; but he isn't that kind. His idea is to last. His outlook isn't rosy—the museum is bound to fall to pieces some day and he knows it, and he himself has more or less fallen to pieces already. Yet there he still sticks, what is left of him. He isn't through yet.

A FRIENDLY SOUL

He's a friendly soul and he longs to please;
    His sins, he is sure, are venial;
      And he's trying to put her quite at her ease
  By being extremely genial.
    She does seem cold,
    But he means no harm.
    His jokes are old
    But his heart is warm.
So he clacks his tongue and he racks his brain,
And her sniffs and snubs are all in vain.

PORTRAIT OF A LADY

Elsie has just got back from an expedition to the Sea Islands. She had had her eye on those islands for a long time, she tells me. They lie off the coast of South Carolina, out of the way of all traffic, and they looked to her like a good hunting ground for African folk-lore. Her ethnological field-work is always taking her off to such places. I suppose that that Englishman, Selous, used to go around studying maps, and questioning natives about the best jungles for lions, in much the same way that Elsie constantly studies our continent, looking for some corner of it that might interest an intelligent person. The parts that are civilization to us, are mere jungle to her: the houses and street cars are like underbrush that she must push through, to get to the places where her quarry is, and where she really wakes up. In between, she lives in New York with us,—she has to,—and conforms to our ways, or to most of them anyhow, just at Stefansson does with the Eskimos: she wears the usual tribal adornments, and beadwork, and skins; she's as dazzling as any other beauty, in her box at the opera; and she sleeps and eats in the family's big stone igloo near Fifth Avenue. An unobservant citizen might almost suppose she was one of us. But every now and then her neglect of some small ceremonial sets our whole tribe to chattering about her, and eyeing her closely, and nodding their hairy coiffures or their tall shiny hats, whispering around their lodge-fires, evenings, that Elsie is queer.

When she went south this time, she first placed herself "in the hands of the whites," as she detachedly puts it: that is to say, she became the guest of a white family on one of the more civilized islands. This was a mistake. They were interested in her plans, and they didn't in the least mean to block them, but they felt it was necessary for them to go around with her everywhere. They wanted to be sure nothing happened,—and Elsie wanted to be sure something did. "They guarded me," she exclaimed, over and over, when she told me this part of it. I got an impression of her tramping off into the wilds, after breakfast, to look around for what she was after, in her business-like way; and of worried hostesses panting along, following her, —in spite of the cold looks they got.

There were also a number of small difficulties. Her smoking, for instance. Her hostesses didn't mind—much; but they had a brother, a clergyman,

who had served in the war with one of those
Y. M. C. A. outfits; and it would upset *him,* they
said. So instead of smoking downstairs, by the fire,
she had to do it up in her room; and also burn
Chinese incense after each smoke, by request.

This clergyman held family prayer-meetings,
regularly, which everybody was supposed to attend; but Elsie did not object. She is always interested in ritual. And the singing was often of
negro spirituals, which she is collecting. She has
a recording phonograph, nowadays, that she takes
around with her, to get them.

This wasn't what she had come down for,
however. It wasn't enough. And not being able
to explore without being "guarded" made the
country no use to her. The game was too shy to
be stalked with a whole crowd of whites. So in
order to make a new entrance, she decided on a
preliminary retreat. She left the islands, went
back to the mainland, and took a room in a
boarding-house.

There was a lady in the neighborhood who once
had collected a few negro tales, but who told Elsie
that the colored folk around there didn't tell them
now. The lady wanted to be obliging, and called
in her cook to make sure; but the cook corrobo-
rated her statement: didn't know any, no ma'am.

Elsie formed the opinion that the cook probably

knew plenty of stories, but would not talk freely to whites. Few or none of them will. She kept on making inquiries, however, as to possible sources, and finally heard about one old negro who was said to be chock-full of folk-lore. Elsie got on his trail. She found him one day in the street, and she soon won him over. He not only told her all he knew, but he stopped a one-armed man going by, —a dirty man with a wheel-barrow full of old bottles—who, the old man said, knew other stories, and who promptly made good, telling several that Elsie took down, while she sat on the curb.

This negro's name was Mr. Jack—at least that is how Elsie speaks of him. He had lost his other arm after a man had shot him up, he said, skylarking. But he could do remarkable things with his remaining one: open an umbrella, for instance. He said that on one of the islands there were people who knew lots of old tales. So Elsie engaged Mr. Jack to go there with her, as guide, and off they sailed, like the owl and the pussy-cat, only with quite other intentions, and they ultimately landed on the beach of the island he'd chosen. There was no wharf. The Sea Islands are primitive. They had to land in the surf. There were two or three natives on the beach, just the way there were when Columbus appeared, but they didn't fall down and worship Elsie—as I should have done.

They just stared, and shuffled away, and were lost in the bush. So Elsie and Mr. Jack pushed on inland, and found a negro with a horse, and Elsie gave him some sticks of tobacco and bright-colored cloth, or whatever currency it is she uses, and added him to her expedition. His name was James Bone, and he had a cart as well as a horse. They all got in this cart and went cruising away into the interior.

It was raining like mad, I forgot to say, but they didn't much mind, and besides it had a result in the end that was lucky for Elsie. There was a store on this island, and James Bone was heading for it, with the idea of depositing Elsie there so she could get shelter. But when they got there, the white man who kept it said his wife was away, and probably wouldn't be back that night because of the rain. Elsie wished to stay anyhow, but he flatly declined to take her in unless his wife came.

After making a silent study of his moral ideas, which he expressed loudly, and writing them down in her notebooks (I hope) for the Folkways Society, Elsie quietly went out in the rain again to continue her travels. It was now dark, however, and Mr. Jack and James Bone were tired. The expedition conferred. James Bone said they could go to some friends of his, named (I think) Peevie, who had a large house with five rooms in it. So they steered for this landmark. But when they arrived, very late, all the five rooms were found to be full. In addition to the whole Peevie family, which was sufficiently numerous, there were several Peevie relations and guests who had come on for a funeral. But James Bone was insistent. He went indoors and stirred them up and made a lot of talk and excitement, and never stopped until the funeral guests rose and went away, in the rain; and with them all the relations except old Aunt Justine and her nieces. These and the regular family somehow packed themselves into three rooms, and gave up the two best to Elsie, who promptly retired. I don't know where Mr. Jack slept. Maybe under the cart.

This cabin was about the most comfortable place Elsie stayed. She could smoke all she wished, she had a fireplace, and the cooking was good. Her two rooms were only six by ten apiece, but all the more cozy. Old Aunt Justine, who at first had not liked it, thawed after a while, and sat around with Elsie and smoked with her and told her old tales. She was a picturesque ancient, Elsie says, and wore a large clean white turban.

Everybody came and told Elsie all the stories they knew. If anyone passed on the road, he was hailed to come in: "Hi, Numph, d'you wanter make a quarter, telling this lady a story?"

"We wouldn't have told you any, though, if you had stayed at the store," James Bone said. "We don't have no traffic with the white folks, only buying or selling. They keep to themselves, and we keep to ourselves, 'cept for that."

Elsie put it all down. "No nexus exists but the economic one between the two groups," she wrote. Then, having exhausted this island, she packed up her notebooks, and she and Mr. Jack put to sea again to visit one other.

This other was an island where Mr. Jack said he had relatives, whom he would love dearly to see again if they were alive. He had lived right over on the mainland without visiting them for about twenty years, until Elsie came along and roused his energies; but he now felt warmed up. When they landed, however, none of his relatives were at all glad to see him. He and Elsie wandered around for a while, getting a chilling reception, until late in the day they met some women who were opening oysters. One of these exclaimed at seeing Mr. Jack, and gave him a great welcome. An old sweetheart, Elsie conjectured. Mr. Jack introduced her. These women gave Elsie a handful of oysters to eat for her supper, and she got out some of her own thick bran cookies which are so good for the stomach, and they sat by the fire and talked together until it was midnight. Then the oyster boat left for the mainland, with Elsie aboard. And luckily there was a man on that boat who knew some valuable stories, so Elsie sat up all night taking them down, by a ship's lamp, as they sailed. The wind was light and it was five hours before they reached port.

She parted with Mr. Jack, on the oyster-dock landing, at dawn. "I stayed wid you to de en'," he said; and afterward mailed her her rubbers.

There is more to this story, about her visiting the Cherokee Indians down there. But I don't remember the Cherokee chapter as well as the old Mr. Jack one. Still I hope this gives some kind of picture of Elsie's real life.

THE DUTIES OF THE CLERGY

In Eastern lands the holiest gents
Are those who live at least expense.
They barely speak, they seek release
From active life in prayer and peace.

But in the Western Hemisphere
A saint must catch the public ear
And dust about and shout and bustle,
Combining holiness and hustle.

WHAT EVERY EMBRYO
KNOWS

There's a woman poet who hymns the role
    Of life in the womb. I've heard her beg,
"Return to your natal source, O soul."
    Return, O Rooster, to the egg.

She sings of the joy of lying curled
    In that supposedly restful lair.
Why, there isn't a sweatshop in the world
    Where they work you half so hard as there.

From gills to lungs, from blobs to toes,
    From poor little specks to eyes and ears,
An embryo hurriedly builds and grows
    Till it's done the work of a million years.

What Every Embryo Knows

Folk who object to toil and care
    Rashly ask for a gruesome doom
When they long to go back. Beware, beware!
    Out of the frying-pan into the womb.

HALF-HEARTED MURDERS

Once upon a time there was a soldier, a stern and splendid leader of men, who had everything to live for, including a beautiful wife. He also had a fat, bloated brother. The brother drank like a fish, and he wasn't jolly about it but maudlin.

The soldier suddenly died. In less than two months that objectionable brother married the widow.

The soldier's son was a high-minded and thoughtful, though rather solemn young man. He had always disliked his fat uncle, and he couldn't understand at all now why his mother had married him.

One night this young man saw his father's ghost. He had never believed there were such things as ghosts, being a skeptical youth, and he was just about bowled over by this experience. The ghost said he'd been murdered by the fat uncle and he was indignant about it. He begged his son to avenge him.

The son stewed and fretted over the matter. He decided to investigate privately just how his father had died. He found that he could get no legal evidence of his uncle's guilt, though he did learn enough to convince himself thoroughly of it.

He couldn't make up his mind what to do. He was not a decisive young man. He couldn't nerve himself up to have it out with his uncle, and yet he couldn't quite bear to let things go on as they were.

He kept getting angrier and angrier all the time at his mother. Marrying that dirty shyster! He went to her room one night and told her plainly that it was a rotten thing for her to have done. He couldn't understand, he said, how any woman who had lost such a husband could turn around and marry right afterward such a slob as his uncle.

While he was scolding her, he heard a sound behind one of the curtains. An old gentleman who had come to the conclusion that this young man was mad, and who thought it was desirable to keep an eye on him, had hid himself there beforehand.

When the young man heard the rustling, and saw a fat form moving behind the curtain, he ran his sword through it. But it wasn't his uncle, as he had hoped, it was only that harmless old gentleman.

He explained as best he could to his mother that it was an accident. He said he had seen something move and had supposed that it was a rat. It wasn't a very brilliant explanation, but somehow the affair was hushed up.

He now felt more bothered than ever. He had been in love for a long time with that old gentleman's daughter. Instead of talking over his troubles with her like a sensible fellow, he had abruptly stopped courting her without a word, after seeing that ghost. She hadn't reproached him, but when she found that on top of deserting her he had killed her old father too, it was more than she could bear and she killed herself. She was found drowned.

That made two deaths so far that were due to this gentlemanly young man's vacillation. Two were not enough. Most men would have pulled themselves together by this time, at least, and have decided either to kill the bad uncle or get out and live somewhere else. Not this young man. He was a bungler by nature, and he couldn't and wouldn't stop bungling.

The girl's brother and his own mother were the next two to die. At a little family fencing match which was given in his honor one evening, his mother drank poison by mistake as she sat looking on. The uncle always kept plenty of poison handy, standing around in odd places, hoping his nephew would drink some, and this was the result. Then while the young man and the girl's brother were fencing, they mortally wounded each other.

That pretty nearly cleaned out the family, let alone their circle of friends. Just before he himself died though, this hesitating youth looked around, and at the very last moment he pulled himself together and finally stabbed his bad uncle.

Ever since Shakespeare dramatized this story, Hamlet has been regarded—especially by actors— as a great tragic figure, simply because on every occasion he had a grand flow of words. He was a wobbler, but God, he was eloquent! A true simian hero.

If Shakespeare had made him a girl I'd have had more sympathy with him. It would be natural for a young lady to feel agitated about sticking a sword in her uncle. Sarah Bernhardt, who loved to feel agitated, put on tights and played Hamlet. Her instinct was sound. It's an excellent role—for a woman.

GRANDFATHER'S THREE LIVES

A great Englishman died a few years ago, little known in America. His name, Sir Charles Dilke. A statesman, a radical, a republican; and a strong solid man.

There is one thing that strikes you about some of these leaders, in England: the number of advantages they have when they're boys, growing up. It gives them a tremendous head-start. Charles Dilke began meeting great men when he was a mere child: the Duke of Wellington, Thackeray, Dickens,—I could name a long list. And he had the close companionship of a grandfather, a man of distinction, who treated him as an equal, and devoted himself to his grandson's development.

A fortunate boy.

Think of other small boys who show signs of fine brains and strong characters. Are they ever introduced to Thackeray or treated as equals? No, they're taught to respect their dull fathers and their fathers' ideas. They are taught not to have any separate ideas of their own. Or at best they run wild with no wise elder friend, like Charles Dilke's.

Here is one of his grandfather's letters. Shows the tone of their friendship. The boy has just won an English Essay Prize, and "they say that parts of my essay were vulgar," he writes. "My special interest," his grandfather answers, "is aroused by the charge of occasional vulgarity. If it be true, it is not improbable that the writer caught the infection from his grandfather. With one half the world, in its judgment of literature and life, vulgarity is the opposite of gentility, and gentility is merely negative, and implies the absence of all character, and, in language, of all idiom, all bone and muscle. . . . You may find in Shakespeare household words and phrases from every condition and walk in life—as much coarseness as you please to look for—anything and everything except gentility and vulgarity. Occasional vulgarity is, therefore, a question on which I refuse to take the opinion of any man not well known to me."

Good for Grandfather! Eh? He was a pretty interesting old boy. He might have been a great man himself, if he could have brought himself up. But Great-grandfather had been in the government's service in England, some position in the Navy Department, or the Admiralty, as they call it. And when his son grew up, he got him a place in the Admiralty too. He meant well, but Grandfather might have done better without.

It gave him a berth, and a chance to lie back and look on. And while that helped to ripen his wisdom, it sapped his initiative.

He had a fine mind; clear, impartial. Strong radical views. He had character, integrity, insight. A man of much weight. But he saw there was much

to be learned and observed about life, and his instinct was to go slow, and quietly study its problems. "Instead," you say, "of immediately solving them like other young men!" But instead, too,— for such was his instinct—of *handling* the problems. He wished to know more and feel wiser before he dealt with them. He had the preparatory attitude.

The trouble with the preparatory attitude is there's no end to it. There is so much to learn in this world that it won't do to wait. If you wait to fit yourself before acting, you never will act. You will somehow lose the habit of acting. Study too conscientiously the one hundred best books on swimming, and of course you'll learn a great deal about it, but you never will swim.

This was Grandfather's type. If he had been kicked out alone into the world and found everyone fighting him, and if he had had to fight back, and fight hard, from his boyhood, it would have taught him the one thing he needed—more force for his powers.

As it was, he remained in the Admiralty. Studying life.

Grandfather was thirty-seven years old when Great-grandfather died. Grandfather had been writing for the magazines for quite a long time,— he was only twenty-six when the *Quarterly Review* editors began to speak highly of him.

He now bought the London *Athenæum*, which, though just born, was dying. Under Grandfather's editorship it became an important authority. It was known all over the world soon. But Grandfather wasn't. He never signed one of his articles, not even pseudonymously. And during the sixteen years in which he had control of the paper, this remarkable man withdrew altogether from general society, in order, he said, to avoid making literary acquaintances which might either prove annoying to him, or be supposed to compromise the integrity of his journal.

That rings hollow, that reason. He doubtless thought it true; but it wasn't. He withdrew from society, probably, because he liked withdrawing. With the gifts of a great man he didn't have a great man's robustness. Some kink in him held him back, and kept him from jousting and tournaments. He should have been psychoanalyzed. It may have been such a small kink.

I doubt if he ever would have married, but it happened quite young. He was under nineteen, and the pretty girl he married still younger. Maybe she married *him*. They had one son, soon after their marriage; but no other children.

I wonder if Grandfather was a case of suppressed personality. It wasn't a weak personality. It would not stay suppressed. But it didn't come out boldly and naturally, and live a full life. Not as full a life as its own wisdom and strength made appropriate. He achieved several things, and they weren't unimportant or small, yet he constantly slighted his life-work; in fact, hardly spoke of it. Modern psychologists do not call this attitude modesty, like our nice naïve fathers. No, they say it comes oftenest from the sexual errors of boyhood. For instance, repression. Or shame at misguided indulgence.

This kind of boyhood is unfortunate, but it

might do small harm if it weren't for the sad sense of guilt with which it stains a man's mind. Men try to forget it, and do: but their subconsciousness never forgets. To be cured, a man must face and remember his past, open-eyed, and see his mistakes philosophically and understand better: understand what we all are, and what human nature is made of, and how it is distorted in youth by a rigid environment. The average moralist or parent won't tell us these things. But until we have learned them, a good many of us feel wicked, and can't put behind us the wretched mistakes of our youth. We don't know enough to regard our young struggles with sympathy. Our ignorance makes us believe we have blackened our souls. And the man who keeps silent and never tells, and hence never learns, goes through the world semi-subdued. Never gets what it owes him.

Was Grandfather Dilke such a case? I've no warrant for saying so. His conscience may have troubled him, possibly, for some quite different reason. He may have secretly hated some relative whom he should have loved. He may have done some small wrong and unfortunately not been found out. But whatever the reason was, he lived an odd, back-groundish life—for a man of his caliber. And his life didn't satisfy him. And this was his fault, not the world's.

The birth of a son, however, in a way gives a man a fresh chance. He decides to live a second and far better life through his son. Whenever a parent feels blue, or is not making good, he immediately declares that his hopes are in his little son anyhow. Then he has a sad, comfortable glow at his own self-effacement. Oh, these shirking fathers! They allow *themselves* to give way to weariness, or be halted by fears; but expect a son, when *he* comes to such moments, to find them quite jolly. He's to make up for the weakness of his father, and carry his own burdens, too!

I regret to say Grandfather Dilke sought relief in this way. Although young, strong, and gifted, he said when his own son was born that he then and there committed all his dreams of achievemet to Baby. Baby was to go out in the world and do his papa honor.

The child was called Wentworth, and it grew up sound, healthy, and kind. But when poor Mr. Dilke bet on Wentworth, he backed the wrong horse. Wentworth didn't have anything in him of the statesman or scholar. He was idle at studies. No head for them. What he liked was athletics. He liked comradeship and enjoying life generally—in a nice way, however. A simple, conservative-minded and limited soul. During his early years in London he was principally known to his friends for never missing a night at the opera. And he was devoted to shooting-parties.

Later on, he became still more trying, it would seem, to his parent. Instead of remaining in his place as a plain disappointment, he began to be prominent; and, stupidly, in just the wrong field. He became a sort of parody of the man his father had hoped he would be. He hadn't the brains, for example, to do anything in the learned *Athenæum*, but he founded the *Gardeners' Chronicle* and the *Agricultural Gazette*. He did well with them, too, which was irritating. He turned out to be a good man of business.

About this time a National Exhibition of some sort was held, and Wentworth was in on it. (It was an exhibition of "art manufacturers.") Then somebody got the idea of repeating it on a large scale and including foreign nations: in fact to make it the first of World's Fairs. So Wentworth and the others met the Prince Consort, to get Royalty's blessing.

The Prince Consort liked the plan immensely. He made it his hobby. Numerous committees were appointed, in true simian style, and amid endless speeches and palaverings, the thing was arranged. Wentworth, except when on shooting-parties, worked hard for it.

This made a great noise; but I doubt if it im-

pressed Mr. Dilke. It was at bottom cheap stuff
which any advertiser or promoter could do. It
sounded well; it made a man prominent, but it
didn't take brains. What Mr. Dilke had hoped or
intended for his son I don't know; perhaps nothing
definite; but he certainly wanted something that
counted. He wanted him to make a contribution
to the needs of mankind. Some achievement in
scholarship, or some hand in the steering of England.

Mr. Dilke was, potentially, anyhow, a big sort
of man, like a nation's prime minister: a publicist,
not a mere showman. And for years he had given
all his thoughts to his son's career. His son had
been the one he first thought of when he woke in
the morning, and the last one that stayed in his
mind when he got into bed. And he hadn't just
mooned around about him, he had worked for his
welfare, planned each step of his education, for
instance, and pondered his plans.

And then the creature grows up to run the
Gardeners' Chronicle, and work for World Fairs.

There were some small advantages. The creature was brought into relations with prominent
men and kings throughout Europe, mostly figure-
heads, perhaps, but not all; and these relations
were destined to be of use to the Dilkes later on.
But it must have seemed awfully silly to Grand-

father to see Wentworth being presented with medals, and honors, and gifts from foreign governments. And as though this weren't enough, Queen

He had medals from potentates.

Victoria wished to make him a baronet! Mr. Dilke, being a radical, was opposed to his taking a title; so Wentworth, who was fifty-one, declined it, like a dutiful child. But the Queen made a personal matter of it, so he had to accept. It seems that he and the Prince Consort had become quite good friends—both being pleasant, gentlemanly, and wooden (at least in some ways), and having in common an innocent love of World Fairs; and this had endeared Wentworth Dilke, more or less, to the Queen. So, after the Prince Consort died, and while she was feeling her grief, she pressed this small title on Wentworth because the Prince liked him.

Wentworth was now a powerfully connected person and a vastly more important man in the public eye than Grandfather was. But he and his father lived in the same house; and, although Mr. Dilke didn't say much, he had his own scale of values; and, measured by any such scale, Wentworth was a great disappointment. Their daily relations were kindly, considering this; but Wentworth knew well, all the time, he was deemed an inferior. When he was out and about, in the public eye, he may have felt like a lord, but when he came home nights he had to check his pride at the door.

Meantime he had married and had two sons; and Charles, the elder, was bright. So Mr. Dilke, the incorrigible, began life all over again. He hadn't been satisfied with his own life, and far less with Wentworth's, but he planned a third career for himself in this promising grandson. He didn't merely take an interest in the child, or just make him his hobby. He centered his whole mind upon him. He made it his business in life to develop that infant—in order that through him he might at last reach the front row.

And this time he won. It looked doubtful at first; Charles was nervous and frail, and hence backward. His mind was too excitable and his health too poor to send him to school. That's a handicap in England; school associations and training count much. However, the boy easily mastered his studies at home, and he often met eminent men who came around to the house, and he made some experiments in literature—in fact, wrote a novel. And when sixteen, he met a beautiful girl, Emilia Strong, whom he worshipped. And he traveled, and talked with his grandfather; and so he grew up.

At eighteen his health grew much better: in fact, grew robust. He immediately entered Cambridge, and there he began a new life. This was a splendid thing for him, in a number of ways. For instance, one of the first things he did was to go in for athletics. He had a flat, narrow chest, sloping shoulders; but the rowing men trained him; and he worked until he became a good oar, and could row on a crew.

He had lived almost entirely with grown-ups before going to college, and was much more mature and well-informed than the fellows he met there. But some parts of his nature had never had a chance to come out; his sense of fun, for example. He now began having good times with boys of his own age. He worked so hard at his rowing that he finally stroked the first crew. And "nobody could make more noise at a boating supper," one of his friends said. He even got into a scrape and was deprived of a scholarship he had won.

All these new ways of Charles—except the scrape, possibly—must have seemed right and normal, and even, perhaps, reassuring to his father, Sir Wentworth. But Sir Wentworth became alarmed lest they shouldn't please Mr. Dilke. He feared Mr. Dilke was going to be disappointed all over again, by a student who found university life too full of pleasure. The unfortunate baronet, therefore, wrote Charles for heaven's sake to be studious.

He need not have worried. Charles became a wonder at studies. And it wasn't just brilliance—it was long, steady hours, plus brains and concentration, that did it. One thing that helped him do so much was that he never wasted time—he used every spare minute for something. He "would even get in ten minutes of work between river and

Hall." He not only became a prize scholar and oarsman, but won walking races; he joined the Volunteers and became a crack rifle shot, and went in for debating.

His votes and speeches in the debates show the trend of his mind, which was balanced yet radical, like his grandfather's, and always progressive. The American Civil War, which was then being fought, was debated; and the undergraduates voted for the Confederate side, three to one. This was the general feeling in England. But Charles was for the North. Again, when Lord Palmerston was helping to start the Greek monarchy, Charles spoke in favor of a Greek republic, in a college debate.

He wrote long letters to his grandfather regularly about studies and politics, and sent him able analyses and criticisms of articles in the *Athenæum*. The old man at first had been rather silent because of the athletics; but as Charles' mind developed, and as he continued winning prizes in studies, Mr. Dilke grew happier and happier. They were forever corresponding, and were on the most affectionate terms.

Then, one day, a telegram came for Charles, and he hurried home. Wentworth was on the lawn, crying. "He lives only to see you," he said.

"I went upstairs," Charles wrote afterward, "and sat down by the sofa on which lay the Grand, looking haggard, but still a noble wreck. I took his hand, and he began to talk of trivial matters. . . . He seemed to be testing his strength, for at last he said: 'I shall be able to talk to-morrow; I may last some weeks; but were it not for the pang that all of you would feel, I should prefer that it should end at once. I have had a good time of it.' "

The next day they had their last talk. Mr. Dilke made his boy a present he had planned for his birthday, and entrusted him with the disposition of his papers and manuscripts. And he told him, "I have nothing more to say but that you have fulfilled—my every hope—beyond all measure—and—I am deeply—grateful."

So he died.

Charles went back to Cambridge and finished his course with the greatest distinction. He then began contributing to the *Athenæum*, and planning to write books. *A History of Radicalism*, for example. *The Effects upon Radicalism of Increased Facility of Communication. Development of the Principle of Love of Country Into That of Love of Man.* In politics he took the Irish Catholic side of the Irish Question; he wrote strongly in favor of removing the political disabilities of women, and he criticized the severity of white men toward natives in the tropics.

He also had a row with his father. Sir Wentworth was vexed because Charles didn't wish to come to his shooting-parties.

When he was twenty-two, Charles made a tour of the world, and recorded his observations in a remarkable book. It was a solid, serious volume, yet written in a vein of high spirits. It dealt with Canada, the United States—East, South, and West —New Zealand, Australia, Ceylon and India; it was a study of what Anglo-Saxons were doing in these great civilizations. Charles mailed his MSS. to England, and Sir Wentworth took it upon himself to correct the proofs, in order to hurry the book through the press. The result was a crop of blunders. But still, it was an enormous success. It ran through three editions rapidly, and brought Charles the friendship of some great men.

Meantime in his twenty-fifth year he was elected to Parliament—at the very election at which Sir Wentworth lost his seat, by the way. Charles advocated laws ('way back in the sixties) to prohibit child labor, to recognize trades unions, and stop the buying of commissions in the army. He advised English workmen not to join the regular political parties, but to start a Labor Party of their own and gain influence that way. He also upset his father a good deal by urging amendments to the game laws. His first speech in Parliament was on some dry, technical subject, but he showed himself so well-informed, so full of detailed knowledge and foreign comparisons, that he was immediately put on a committee and began to make his way in the House.

It's interesting to look back and see how able men get their start.

In his twenty-eighth year this able man got into frightful hot water. He said publicly that a miserable moral and political tone resulted from the nation's retaining a lot of sinecure offices—Hereditary Grand Falconer, and all that sort of thing. He pointed out that the Duke of Edinburgh had been given a naval command without much naval training, and he advocated promotion by merit instead of by claims due to birth. He allowed himself to criticize some large grants of money to the monarchy. His remarks indicated that theoretically he preferred a republic. For this he was denounced by the papers, and socially shunned. He was accused of disloyalty and treason, with the greatest heat, everywhere. His name was a by-word. The Prince of Wales happened about this time to get very ill, and this added still further to the anger men felt at Charles Dilke.

He didn't back down. He went out and made speeches to workmen, repeating his anti-King criticisms. There was rioting by Tory roughs—iron bars thrown—men injured and killed. Crowds collected who swore that Dilke should not get away alive from the hall. He waited till the excitement was hottest, then came out the main door alone, stood quietly looking at them, lit a cigar, and walked off.

He did, however, gradually calm down the nation in one way, by showing them that, though he objected to monarchical errors, he didn't wish to upset the monarchy while it suited the people. He thought it absurd, but it would be still more absurd to upset it—that is to say, while those governed wanted it. This attitude, and time (several years of it) slowly stilled the excitement. The net result was to make this man a notable and recognized power.

His power kept growing. His influence was great in the House. His views were strong, but reasoned and sane, and his industry endless. He was now forty-two. Gladstone, with whom he tilted at first, picked him as his successor. It looked as though this great progressive would be premier of England.

Then, in a night, the Fates crushed him. Returning home from a dinner in his honor, he found a letter there, waiting.

It said that the wife of a member of Parliament had confessed to her husband that she had been unfaithful to him with Charles Dilke soon after her marriage.

This, of course, meant a scandal. And a scandal meant he couldn't be premier. He couldn't even sit in the Cabinet. His career was destroyed.

Sir Charles (as he now was) had been married, but his wife had soon died. After ten years as a widower, he had become engaged to Emilia Strong —you remember?—the same Emilia whom he had worshipped when he was sixteen. (She had been married, too, in the meantime, but she now was a widow.) His principal concern with this blow was not to let it hurt her. He sent her the news, told her he was innocent, and added, "I feel this may kill you—and it will kill me, either if it kills you or if you don't believe me."

She stood by him, married him. They had nineteen years of each other. He was sixty-one when she died in his arms. He lived to be sixty-eight.

He never could clear his name of the scandal, though he took it to court. They failed to show he was guilty, but he couldn't *prove* that he wasn't. So he never was premier, and he never again sat in the Cabinet.

His friends said his whole career showed that the scandal was false. They stood by him strongly. But the People, whom he would have served with such courage, did not.

MIGHT AND RIGHT

Might and Right are always fighting.
In our youth it seems exciting.
Right is always nearly winning.
Might can hardly keep from grinning.

HUME, THE GEORGE BERNARD SHAW OF HIS TIME

✲

Every once in a while a man is born with a brilliant and athletic mind. Alexander Hamilton had such a mind. He used it to make himself a general and a statesman, and he planned our government with it. George Bernard Shaw has such a mind. Not being a man of action, like Hamilton, he became a critic and commentator—the kind of man who loves to explain things to everybody. It's a valuable power to have, and Shaw has made people pay for it.

There was a man born in 1711 who was the Shaw of his time, David Hume. Like Shaw, he had the power of grasping and piercing the important ideas of his age, and a brilliantly clear way of writing about them. Like Shaw, he was industrious and used his ability to make a great deal of money. Like Shaw, he wasn't much of a lover, but he was happy enough in his own way. He also had a good sense of humor, though he wasn't as witty as Shaw. He was a more responsible type. He was a thrifty hard-headed man who was concerned for his health, and who cared a good deal both for money and applause and who got them.

In spite of having one of the most brilliant minds of his day Hume had a hard time getting started in life. Perhaps that was why he was so greedy even after he became old and successful. In Edinburgh, where he was born, he had a try at the law. In Bristol he was a clerk in the counting house of a merchant. He didn't like either of these occupations. He said his clerkship was "stifling." When he was twenty-three, his father gave him a small allowance and sent him to France, to study in a Jesuit institution, the famous La Flèche.

The Jesuits found that he had a good mind and they sharpened it. They also, however, directed it into philosophical channels. After three years he went back to Scotland and began to write books. Although he still was full of youthful frailties, being only twenty-six years of age, his first book was a complete picture and survey of Man. He called it a *Treatise of Human Nature*. It was in a philosophical vein. It got no welcome, it brought him no money, it gave him no fame. He wrote several more with no better results. He kept this up till he was forty.

In all these books Hume used his keen and analytical mind to pull apart and belittle the philosophies of his predecessors. They were radical books and considered in those days irreligious. This gradually made him obnoxious to conservative men.

After sticking to such subjects as miracles and morals for years, and never getting anywhere at all, he wrote a book about politics. This got a better reception. Hume tasted success.

It didn't teach him his lesson at first—the lesson of what he could best use his gifts for. Instead he tried to use his success to become a professor of logic. If he could only get himself appointed professor of logic, he thought, he could continue to deal with philosophy, and keep on the wrong track. But he failed. He wasn't regarded as good enough for this professorship.

At the age of forty-one he got a job as a librarian instead. This gave him a small but regular salary, and freed him from worry. And while browsing around in this library and examining its old papers and records, his mind was again directed, by chance, into political channels. He decided to write a history of England.

Opportunity, which had knocked on his door before, now knocked again, and this man who had always had it in him to write a great history, but who had never tried and never even thought of trying any such task, at last ceased to busy himself with his dusty debates about nothing, and sat down to compose the first volume of a *History of England*.

This first volume was angrily received, but for a curious reason. The public in those days, although conservative in religion, were free-thinkers in politics. Hume had written as a free-thinker on religion, but in politics he was a Tory. He sympathized with Charles I instead of with Cromwell. It was about a hundred years since Charles had been beheaded, but Hume was denounced on all hands.

He was so discouraged that he half-thought of changing his name and moving to France. But the outbreak of war made this impracticable, and besides he was afraid that if he went to France the charming Comtesse de Boufflers might marry him. So he remained shut up in his library and composed Volume Two.

This at last brought him fame. He hadn't changed his conservative political views, he was a cheerfully obstinate man, but people began to appreciate him. He was writing a new kind of history. It wasn't a mere chronicle of statesmen and kings and their battles. It was a history of the habits and customs of the people, and of the ways men earned money, and how much their food and drink cost them and what kinds of taxes they paid.

He described what the world at large was like in each era, to give a proper setting to England. And he did this in a remarkably easy and readable style.

After that Hume was regarded as one of the great men of Europe. He who had been refused a professorship was now showered with honors. He became rich, respected, and very much pleased with himself. More pleased perhaps, than if he hadn't bungled along those wrong paths first.

PORTRAIT OF AN ARTIST

A sober man named Gideon Deems
Was handicapped by mighty themes.
He was a painter with a tart
And moralistic sense of art,
Not ill-adapted to portray
The life he led from day to day.
He might have done an aquarelle
Of pickled snowdrops very well,
Or cowsheds where the sparrow lingers,

Or lambrequins, or lady-fingers.
But subjects which he should have prized
The soul of Gideon Deems despised.
He loved to labor in the toils
Of doing deities in oils.
He bravely let his fancies dwell
In heavens that looked to him like hell.
And many a night when he'd designed
A God of some indecent kind,
Both oversexed and undersouled,
The blood of Gideon Deems ran cold.

A SOLDIER PHILOSOPHER

Socrates was a hardy old soldier, who had endured frozen trenches and fought coolly in battles, and who kept plugging along like a bulldog when the army was forced to retreat. He was built like a bulldog. Big husky shoulders, and a snub-nosed, honest face.

He was also an argumentative man who was interested in moral ideas. He had a powerful mind that dug deep into the heart of an argument, and he never was satisfied until he reached a blunt, forceful answer.

He himself didn't think he was a wise man except in one respect: he did see that it was the simplest things which fooled people worst. His other strong point was that he didn't sit in a study and formulate principles. He worked them out by having mental tussles with the people he met in the street. And instead of then living by his principles in quiet seclusion, which is the safe course that so many great thinkers adopt, Socrates shouldered his way with his into the market-place and lived by them there, which resulted at last in his having to die for them too.

Nobody wanted him to die. The big politicians wanted to get rid of him, because he kept showing them up, but banishment would have met their requirements. He felt that it didn't meet his. He wasn't going to surrender and go off into exile to please them. So this uncouth and plain-thinking hero stuck to his guns and drank hemlock.

MRS. P'S SIDE OF IT

So Prometheus, the Titan, seeing the great need that man had of fire, risked all and set out for Olympus, and brought thence the flame.

And warmth, comfort, art and inventions spread over the world.

But as to Prometheus, he was seized by the gods, in their wrath, and chained to a rock in the Scythian wilds, by the sea. There no ear heard his cries. There he raged on alone, year by year, with his eyelids cut off, while cold-hearted vultures with great beaks like horns tore his flesh.

It is interesting to think that Prometheus, who is a hero to us, may have been regarded quite differently by his contemporaries. Some thought of him, maybe, as a sort of social settlement worker, living among men to improve them, in a sleek, earnest spirit. Some as a common adventurer. Others a radical.

As a matter of fact. he was probably very much like the rest of us.

The records seem to indicate he was a well-to-do prominent citizen, who was active in getting the world of his day straightened out. I imagine him

going around town, in the real-estate business, a
substantial, respected man, planning highways and
harbor facilities. Then he gets this idea, about
bringing down fire from heaven. At first he dis-
misses it. But he thinks about the advantages of
fire, and begins to believe he could get it. He starts
talking to others about it. Everyone laughs. His fellow business-men call him a visionary. He defends
his plan, and tries to explain why it's perfectly
practicable, but he does it so warmly they begin to
lose some of their trust in him. The word goes
around not to elect him to the Chamber of Commerce. The solid men of the community begin to
avoid him. A famous university silently changes
its plans, and decides not to give Mr. Prometheus
that LL.D. degree. And finally one of his friends
pays him a call, after dark, and bluntly and worriedly warns him he's queering himself.

Prometheus goes upstairs, indignant, to talk to
his wife. He doesn't tell her anything about the
community's criticisms, but he describes all over
again what a boon fire would be to mankind. After
an hour of this he has reassured himself. His wife
is quite thrilled. She says he is wonderful, and no
one ever had such a husband.

But she says it sounds awfully dangerous.

"Well," he owns, "there's *some* risk, but we
ought to look at it impersonally."

Mrs. P's Side of It

She says: "Looking at it quite impersonally, I think you had better not do it."

"*What?*" he shouts; "don't you realize what a tremendous help fire would—"

"Oh *yes*, dear," she says: "the plan's *perfect*. But *you* shouldn't go. You have such important work to attend to, here at home, without that. Some younger, less valuable person—"

"Ah, my dear," Prometheus laughs, "you're like everyone else. You want to see the world helped,

and wars won, whatever the cost; but you don't want either me or you to pay any part of the price. You think all dangerous work should be done by some other woman's husband."

Mrs. Prometheus purses her lips, and her face

becomes obstinate. "I don't think *any* married man has a right to take such risks," she observes.

"Well, you ought to hear what the single men say about that," he retorts. "It's pretty thick to expect them to die, they say, for other men's wives."

Mrs. Prometheus shrugs and doesn't bother to comment on that point of view. Instead, she says tactfully that she sees Prometheus has set his heart upon going, and she wants him to feel perfectly free to do just what he likes. Only there are certain practical matters that one must consider. There's the mortgage, and the laundress—unless he'd like to have her do the washing herself, which she'd be glad to do only he never took those stones out of her way, in the brook—and there's the bill for that last set of bear-skins that she got for the windows; and she doesn't see exactly how she can keep the home up by herself, if he is to wander around neglecting his real-estate business.

He says he won't be chained by his business.

She reminds him that she has already explained he's perfectly free. But she just wants to know how he wishes her to arrange in his absence.

"Very well, then," he blazes out, "I will give up my plan: let it go! let men go to the devil! I'm a prisoner, that's what it comes to. Like all married men. There isn't a damn one of us that's allowed to do what the world needs, or anything fine and unselfish."

She says that's unjust. She'd *love* to have him be a great hero, and she always has said so, but she doesn't see why he can't be one without leaving his wife.

Prometheus gets up with a groan and walks out of the house, leaving her feeling injured and won-

Pegged down

dering at the hardness of men. And he stamps up and down the yard, working himself up into a state, and filling his mind with dark pictures. Must every married man sit at home with his wife in his arms, yearning for roving and achievement, but yearning in vain? Pegged down, with a baby as a peg, and a mortgage as jailer. Must every young fellow choose between a fiancée and adventure?

Even when he does choose adventure, they won't let him alone. There will always be some girl at a window as he passes by, who will tempt him to stop and play dolls with her, and stay indoors for keeps,

and wrestle with a mortgage for exercise, and give up the road. Prometheus swears. He tries to imagine what our epics would be like if wives wrote them: what heroes they'd sing. Tidy, amiable, hearthstone heroes, who'd always wind up the clock regularly, and never invent dangerous airplanes or seek the North Pole. Ulysses knitting sweaters by the fireside. George Washington feeding canaries. . . .

Well, Prometheus gives in, of course, and abandons his plan, as millions of others have done, after talks with their wives. But there is another great force besides wives in the world.

It happened, as you know, that Prometheus didn't get on well with Zeus. They had different ideas as to how the world should be arranged. Prometheus had more experience, but Zeus had the power. Rivalry, combined with dislike,—that is the great force I speak of. Zeus didn't wish men to have fire. That was enough for Prometheus. He told himself how incompetent Zeus was to manage the world, how selfish he was, how indifferent to men's need of fire. And that was what braced him,

at last, to escape from his wife, and bring down an ember from heaven, and bestow it upon men.

"General Rejoicing on Earth," said the newspapers, when the deed had been done. To get anything from heaven seemed as remarkable then as it would now. Prometheus having accomplished something was immediately ranked as a hero. The Chamber of Commerce still privately thought he had been rather wild, but after a debate on the subject they gave him a dinner. He was also presented with a loving cup and the keys of the city. (He had no use for either, but those primitive men thought them honors.) And after the public reception Prometheus went home, and had another reception behind closed doors from Mrs. Prometheus, who had had to sell preserves and take in sewing while he was away.

Meanwhile everybody was using this newfangled thing, fire, except old men who were set in their ways and who said it was dangerous. And presently men found it *was* dangerous. It wasn't just a question of scorched fingers—it burned out two caves. It roasted the toes of a lady who went to sleep while cooking sliced elephant. And although Prometheus had warned them and warned them about being careless, and had shown them exactly how to use it, he was blamed for each burn.

It was owing to this that the gods discovered what he had done. A volley of terrible thunderclaps at once shook the skies, and Zeus had Prometheus arrested. He was led off to Scythia—the Siberia of those times—without trial, and the police left him chained to a rock there, and hurried back home. And everybody sympathized greatly with Mrs. Prometheus, for having a husband who had willfully disgraced his poor wife. And they tried to be nice to her, but of course she was under a cloud, and had to take in more sewing than ever, and was never asked out. And a year or two later some books were written, psychoanalyzing Prometheus; and a professor who had made a study of the economic interpretation of heroes wrote an interesting paper discussing his probable profits.

So his great deed ended in confusion. Like other great deeds. All he got was a tumult of mixed praise and blame from the crowd; and in his dark moments he must have felt completely discouraged, and wished that he'd just lived along in comfort and minded his business.

His friend, who had warned him originally, thought of him at times. He used to sit at home and feel glad that for his part he'd kept out of it. Then he would stir up the fire in his grate and comfortably get into bed, and forget about Prometheus, facing the winds and the vulture.

HE LEARNED TO ROOST
ON A REEF

One of the Greeks who were carried off to Rome in the old days, to serve the Romans as slaves, was a sickly and extremely hot-tempered man, whose name was Epictetus.

The Roman whom he was compelled to serve was a friend and companion of Nero's. A man who was a slave to any of that crowd was up against a tough gang.

On his days off, Epictetus used to go and listen to lectures, especially to lectures by some mental healers who called themselves Stoics. They gave him the idea that no matter what was done to his body his mind was free and his own; and that it was in anyone's power, even a slave's, to be noble and calm—in his mind.

Later on, after his master had freed him, he gave lectures himself. Owing to the indignities he had borne, some of his teachings were a little one-sided, but his feelings were deep and sincere. Furthermore he knew from his own experience that stoi-

cism could be of great help to those who were sick
or unfortunate, especially if they also were irri-
table; and he had such a clear and striking way of
telling his story that people crowded to hear him.

Epictetus believed and declared that everyone
could learn to keep cool, and that anyone was a
fool if he didn't. A fool. Which of us would lie
naked in the gutter, he asked, and invite those who
passed by to kick his body or trample upon him?
We take better care than that of our bodies. Then
why, he demanded, don't we take more care of our
inner selves? Why do we give mean or stupid persons the run of our minds, and let them trample
on them and wound us? Epictetus scornfully told
his hearers they didn't have to do that.

Unlike many mental healers, however, the results he expected were small, for he had had to
practice what he preached, and this had made him
a realist. In one of his talks, for example, he said:
"Reckon the days in which you have not been
angry. I used to be angry every day, then every
other day, then every third or fourth day."

He added that if a man ever managed to go as
many as thirty days without getting angry, he
ought to give thanks to God.

He must have had plenty of things to get angry
about during his slavehood. They say that his
master broke his leg for him one day, and lamed

him for life. Whether or not this was how it happened, Epictetus was lame. But he didn't allow that to bother him. "Disease," he said, "is an impediment to the body but not to the will—unless the will itself chooses." On this basis he regarded his lameness merely as a bit of hard luck for his leg.

Epictetus was now generally accepted as a full-fledged Philosopher. From this time on, his reputation grew rapidly, but he himself didn't. Rome was full of Philosophers. When the Emperor Domitian was on the throne he got sick and tired of them. They just sat around and talked and made a good thing out of it. They didn't do any work. They said they were performing a useful service by doing sound thinking, but they all disagreed with each other about nearly everything, and very few of them regarded any of the others as sound. The only thing they were unanimous about was in disliking the Emperor. Domitian at last had a clean-up, and drove the whole crowd out of town.

Epictetus left with the others, but his development had come to a standstill, he was a confirmed talker now, and as soon as he could he opened a new office in the Epirus. Business was good there, he had numerous disciples who venerated him highly, and he kept talking away about stoicism for the rest of his life.

He was and he is a great figure, and his books are still read, but, for anyone who is down on his luck and is having a hard time to live, there's more honest-to-God inspiration in Robinson Crusoe. Epictetus didn't get anywhere. Or rather he didn't keep going. He learned how to bear hardship and pain, but he did nothing else. As a lecturer to other men on the subject of how to be stoical, he begins to sound, after a while, like an iron-hearted old maid.

He conquered misfortune. When he was wrecked on a rocky shore, so to speak, he learned how to camp out there. He learned, and he tried to teach others, how to roost on a reef. But he was a Greek, not a Viking. He didn't try to patch up his ship again and put back to sea.

PORTRAIT OF A STRANGER

He always was stopping, in a quiet, considering attitude, with his broad head on one side, to take a fresh look at the world. He wasn't a poet and he didn't go around talking about it, but he had an affection for the place—he regarded it all as his home. At sea he would stand fascinated for hours at a time at the rail, getting the feel of the great mass beneath him—the strong, living ocean. Or he would sit on a beach half the day, watching the waves, one by one, while his horse pawed the sand restlessly and stared at the waters. It was the same when he went inland: he understood plains. I joined him once in Nebraska, 'way off on a great, bare, flat prairie. He had left his Eastern home and gone to work there, to live under those skies.

He liked hills too, and rivers, and winds. Each had something to tell him. He even liked deserts; he disappeared into one once for three years. In short, he seemed glad he was born on this particular earth. He traveled about and looked it all over; not the cities so much, which he seemed to regard as warts on its surface, but the old earth itself. He had an idea something could be made of it, if men ever learned.

His attitude toward men was not that of a fellow-being, exactly, though he didn't look down on them, like a teacher, or ruler, or general; he pondered their history the way anthropologists do. He thought of men as a species, trying to tenant the planet the best way they could: a gifted, bewildered, pathetic, mysterious race. He talked of mankind as them, not as us. He hoped for great things of them; or rather it wasn't exactly hope; it wasn't an emotion at all; it was more a serene expectation that they would some day succeed. In mastering their fears, for example, and understanding their natures; and in being more generous in their quarrels, less cheap in their follies. Meantime he smiled at most of their barbarities—including his own.

This wasn't aloofness precisely. It was the consciousness, rather, of a man's dual role. Part of the time he was one of this race himself, part of the time he looked on. He seemed to think everyone did this. Well, of course, many do. But the way that he did it was a little different from the usual observer's. Politicians are observers, for instance, but they are concerned with the present; they deal with men as they are; but he didn't. His eye was on our future.

Imagine a lot of babies who know perfectly well they will some day grow up, but who meantime are helpless to do anything much about it but wait— that was how he regarded himself and other intelligent persons.

The simile is imperfect. Babies do grow up, but we don't; we must leave our hopes of better things to future generations and centuries. But he never felt cheated about this: a little regretful, that's all.

Meanwhile any signs that human beings were maturing encouraged him. He liked to see a man behave sensibly, even if it were only about some insignificant decision or habit. And when a whole nation did some sensible act, it gave him a deep satisfaction. He wasn't the kind of man to be thrilled, but he felt a thrill at such moments.

He liked to discuss the quirks and stupidities he found in his own nature, and plan how to civilize a few of his obstinate instincts. He laughed when he couldn't—at the ways his sloth tricked him for instance, or at his ego's unphilosophic indignation over undue demands on it.

He rarely censured anyone but himself; never a body of people. His whole attention went into trying to understand their misdoings. Modern lynchings depressed him more than anything else; but, instead of denouncing them, he tried (vainly) to get at the why of them, like a scientist studying some cruel and loathsome disease. The only kind of men he ever really lost his temper about were cynical leaders who seemed to regard men as cattle, and who cajoled and then bled their followers; or, in business, exploited them.

In his personal relations with people he was always doing kind things, but he was always surprised if anyone inferred from this that he was their friend. He simply had an instinct for helping to straighten things out. The big tangles were not his affair—he had learned to take that for granted—but any small difficulty, any hardship or friction or quarrel, that he could smooth he always would try to, no matter how much it cost.

He never found anyone stuck in a bog without trying to give them a lift. Sometimes this meant money, sometimes merely undoing kinks. He would try to explain parent and child to each other, or an employer and worker, or persons of different temperaments, religions, or political faiths. He would go on difficult errands, write letters, plan, argue, make gifts, all from this impersonal desire to see things working better.

There was one thing about this—he was generous only in his own way. He hated to be asked any favor. He was too busy carrying the burdens he had shouldered of his own accord. Hardly anyone understood he was impersonal—they thought

what he did was for them. They would then become emotionally grateful. This made him uneasy.
He tried to be considerate, he didn't repulse them;
but he didn't respond; he simply withdrew as fast
as he decently could, and let their feelings die out.

Even people who were cool and impersonal by
nature themselves, would become moved by what
they supposed must be his feelings for them, and
would speak of his warm-hearted loyalty and his
wonderful friendship. Then he would look rather
guilty, for he didn't have those feelings at all. He
usually liked them, and remembered them, or
most of them anyhow; yet in one way he didn't
care if he never saw them again.

He had friends whom he loved, but they were
few, and he never told them he loved them. It
was as unnatural to him to speak of such feelings,
while friends were alive, as it would have been to
dig up the interlacing roots of twin plants. He
seemed to think his friends ought to understand
without any talk about it—understand by his
actions, I suppose. But how could they? They saw
him ready to do things for everybody as well as
his friends.

According to some of his enemies, he had no
heart at all, only an inexplicable interest in human
affairs, like a visitor from some other planet,
curious and kind, but remote. Perhaps he was

remote in a sense. He belonged in the future. He naturally seemed like a stranger to us of the present.

FROM A BLEAK GEORGIAN
MANSION

Parnell seemed more like an English gentleman than an Irish one. His behavior wasn't in any way Celtic and he had no Irish accent. His mother was an American girl. His father was an Irish aristocrat.

The boy's home was a bleak Georgian mansion in Ireland, set among huge silver firs. He was educated at Cambridge in England. He grew up to be a reserved and self-sufficient young man, and when he visited America he took a critical attitude toward our celebrities. President Grant, he said, was "a vulgar old dog."

Unexpectedly enough, Parnell threw himself into the Irish cause, and not only that but after a while he became its chief leader. He had a stern and proud nature, and he wouldn't and didn't lift his finger to gain popularity; he won the leadership by working single-mindedly to set Ireland free.

Working for Ireland took courage in those days, but he had plenty of it, and he had ability too. He forced England to grant to his countrymen one liberty after another, and they loved and revered him for doing it. So much so, that everyone called him the Uncrowned King of Ireland.

Then, in the midst of his efforts, his followers turned on him. Their gratitude to him changed to hatred, and they struck him down.

Their reason was that he had become the lover of another man's wife.

This lady was the sister of an English Field-Marshal. Her husband was a despicable Irishman who cared nothing for her. In all the years since their wedding he had spent only forty nights in their home. On one of his visits he talked about his leader, a lonely man named Parnell.

Parnell, who was a member of the House of Commons, was living in lodgings in London. His whole time was spent on his work. He never went out to parties. But the things which she heard about him interested that lady so much that she invited him to come to her house. For some reason he went, and they met. At the very first glance they exchanged they fell deeply in love.

He was a preoccupied bachelor. He had always felt that he had no time for women. She was a deserted woman who was trying to live a society life for want of a realer one. They were swept off their feet by each other.

Little as either of them liked the idea of an irregular union, they were utterly unable to keep apart. They did not even try. If she could have got a divorce it would have left them free to marry, for neither of them was a Catholic, but she knew that her husband wouldn't consent. She devoted herself to working for Ireland—so as to be with Parnell.

Her husband soon found them out. He kept still about it. His hope was that Parnell would reward him with some political plum.

Parnell didn't.

This went on for years. At last the husband showed Parnell up in a sensational way by taking the case into court, where he got a divorce. The lovers then thankfully married.

The scandal of this divorce case, however, set the mob at their heels. The women of Ireland had worshipped Parnell. They now were wrathful and bitter.

The final scene when his followers took his leadership from him was tragic. They hooted the haggard, silent figure of the man who had done so much for them. They screamed lewd abuse at his wife, which dealt his heart deadly wounds.

He was only forty-five, but soon after they broke him he died.

From a Bleak Georgian Mansion

And years later, the woman whom this reticent hero had loved, and for whom he had sacrificed his career and his life, sold his love letters.

STORY OF A FARMER

There once was a tall husky fellow, big hands and feet; not much education. (Though he came of a fairly good family.) He had very bad teeth. His father had left him a farm, and that was his great interest—farming. He had the kind of feeling about farming that a good shoemaker has about shoes. Of course, he complained more or less, and felt dissatisfied and discouraged, and threatened to give up his farm when things went badly. But there was nothing else he could have willingly turned to; and he was never weary of experimenting with different ways of planting his crops.

He was a sound-thinking man, and men trusted him. He grew prominent. Held some offices. As a result, when he was forty-three he had to go away from home for some years. This was while he was managing an army. And I ought to explain that it was a hard army to manage. It was not only badly equipped and poorly trained, but sometimes the men would run away in the midst of a battle. That made this man angry. He was ordinarily composed and benign in his manner, but when he saw the soldiers showing fear he used to become violently aroused, and would swear at them and strike them. His nature loathed cowardice. He cared nothing for danger himself, perhaps because of his teeth, and he couldn't understand why these other men dreaded to die.

All his life, when he was at table with others, he used to sit there in silence, drumming on the cloth with his fork. He seldom joked. He was hardly ever playful. People said he was too dignified, too solemn. Well! one isn't apt to be a comedian, precisely, with toothache. He was only twenty-two when he began having his teeth pulled, they tortured him so; and when he began to use false ones they fitted him badly.

Imagine him dressing for dinner—fresh linen, clean shaved, spick and span in good clothes—and then he opens a drawer and there are those teeth. He puts them in his mouth and goes slowly downstairs, joggling them about with his tongue, trying to get them to set right. What kind of mood would he be in when dinner was served and when he had to sit there and be bruised by each mouthful in secret? At least it was probably in secret—there were usually guests, and I don't suppose he took the whole table into his confidence, or opened his mouth and whipped them out when trying to eat his first walnut and threw the whole set into the fireplace, crying "Damn those teeth, I am starving!"

About this army again. He didn't want to manage it. He had had quite a liking for military work, as a youth, and had even gone on a small expedition to see active service, though his mother had

interfered all she could, and tried hard to prevent him. But as this was all the experience he ever had had, and as he had never studied warfare, he didn't know anything about handling large bodies of troops.

However, he had a clear mind and a good natural insight; and in spite of his ignorance, of which he was painfully conscious, he managed to win the war, and then thankfully returned to his farm. He went back with enthusiasm. He had been away for eight years altogether, and for six of those years he did not once set foot on his fields. He had found time, however, in between whiles, to talk with the farmers in the northerly parts of his country, and collect new ideas. He now began to experiment with plaster of Paris and powdered stone as fertilizers. He tried clover, rye, peas, oats and carrots to strengthen his land. He tried mud. He planted potatoes with manure, and potatoes without, and noted exactly what the difference was in the yield. His diary speaks of the chinch bugs attacking his corn, and of the mean way the rain had of passing by on the other side of the river, falling generously there, while "not enough fell here to wet a handkerchief." He laboriously calculated the number of seed in a pound (this retired Commander!) and found the red clover had 71,000, timothy 298,000 and barley 8,925.

He saw lots of people. And he was laid up occasionally with malaria, and fever and ague. And he was called upon to help frame a constitution for his little nation. A busy period. He had an attack of rheumatism, too, which lasted over six months, and it was sometimes so bad he could hardly raise his hand to his head or turn over in bed. And when the national constitution had been adopted they elected him president. That meant a lot of outside work for another eight years.

Some of this work he hated. He hated speech-making for instance. At his inauguration he was so agitated and embarrassed that men saw he trembled, and when he read his speech his voice was almost too low to be heard. He was always very conscious of having a poor education, and being a bad speller and so forth. But the people didn't care about that, much: they trusted his judgment, and admired the man's goodness and spirit.

A sculptor was sent to make a statue of him, late in his life. He couldn't get him to pose satisfactorily. No noble attitudes. In vain did the sculptor talk about state affairs and that war. Such things did not stir him. He remained either stiff or relaxed. But one day they were out on the farm together; and as this man watched his live-stock, he unconsciously took a fine, alive attitude. So the sculptor made a statue of him that way; and that statue is famous.

In spite of his usual benignity, this man had a temper. He used to get very sore and warm at times, when unfairly criticized. At one of his cabinet meetings, for instance, says a contemporary, he became "much inflamed, got into one of those passions when he cannot command himself,

ran on much on the personal abuse which had been
bestowed on him [and said] that by God he had
rather be in his grave than in his present situation.
That he had rather be on his farm than to be made
emperor of the world, and yet that they were
charging him with wanting to be a king. That that
rascal Freneau sent him three of his papers every
day, as if he thought he would become the distribu-
tor of his papers; that he could see nothing in this
but an impudent design to insult him," etc., etc.
Poor, stung human being; with all his serenity
gone!

A great portrait-painter said of him that his
features were indicative of the strongest and most
ungovernable passions; and had he been born in
the forests, it was his opinion that he would have
been the fiercest man among the savage tribes.

This was the temperament that smoldered in
him: the lurking flame that he had to live with
daily. But by reflection and resolution he obtained
a firm ascendancy over it.

One night when he was sixty-seven years old
he woke up at about two in the morning feeling
very unwell. He had had a sore throat, and now he
couldn't swallow; felt suffocated. A miserable feeling. His wife would have got up to call a servant;
but he wouldn't allow her to do it lest she should
catch cold. He lay there for four hours in the cold

bedroom, his body in a chill, before receiving any attention or before even a fire was lighted. Then they sent for the doctors. They bled the old hero three times, taking the last time a quart. He was physically a vigorous man, but this weakened him greatly. "I find I am going," he said. He was in great pain, and said, "Doctor, I die hard." A little later he added: "I feel I am going. I thank you for your attention, you had better not take any more trouble about me, but let me go off quietly." His breathing became much easier just at the end.

Did Washington look back at his life as he lay there, and what did he think of it? That his farming had been interesting though difficult, and much interrupted? That his fellow-men had really asked a good many sacrifices of him, and not left him nearly as much time as he wished for his fields? Or did he think that in death he would at least have no more trouble with teeth? A set of dental instruments was found in one of his drawers after the funeral. In others were memoranda about affairs of state he had worked at, and various kinds of plows he had tried, and his farming accounts.

A NOTE ON THE TYPE IN WHICH THIS BOOK IS SET

The text of this book was set on the linotype in Baskerville. The punches for this face were cut under the supervision of George W. Jones, an eminent English printer. Linotype Baskerville is a facsimile cutting from type cast from the original matrices of a face designed by John Baskerville. The original face was the forerunner of the "modern" group of type faces. ¶ John Baskerville (1706-75), of Birmingham, England, a writing-master, with a special renown for cutting inscriptions in stone, began experimenting about 1750 with punch-cutting and making typographical material. It was not until 1757 that he published his first work, a Virgil in royal quarto, with great-primer letters. This was followed by his famous editions of Milton, the Bible, the Book of Common Prayer, and several Latin classic authors. His types, at first criticized as unnecessarily slender, delicate, and feminine, in time were recognized as both distinct and elegant, and both his types and his printing were greatly admired. Printers, however, preferred the stronger types of Caslon, and Baskerville before his death repented of having attempted the business of printing. For four years after his death his widow continued to conduct his business. She then sold all his punches and matrices to the Société Littéraire-typographique, which used some of the types for the sumptuous Kehl edition of Vol-taire's works in seventy volumes.—

COMPOSED, PRINTED, AND BOUND
BY H. WOLFF, NEW YORK. PAPER
MADE BY S. D. WARREN
CO., BOSTON